D0616379

A Ministry Anyone Could

A Study of 2 Corinthians 1–7

From the Bible-Teaching Ministry of

CHARLES R. SWINDOLL

INSIGHT FOR LIVING

Charles R. Swindoll graduated in 1963 from Dallas Theological Seminary, where he now serves as the school's chancellor, helping to prepare a new generation of men and women for the ministry. Chuck has served in pastorates in three states: Massachusetts, Texas, and California, including almost twenty-three years at the First Evangelical Free Church in Fullerton, California. He is currently senior pastor of Stonebriar Community Church in Frisco, Texas, north of Dallas. His sermon messages have been aired over radio since 1979 as the *Insight for Living* broadcast. A best-selling author, he has written numerous books and booklets on many subjects.

Based on the outlines, charts, and transcripts of Charles. R. Swindoll's sermons, the study guide text was written by Ken Gire, a graduate of Texas Christian University and Dallas Theological Seminary. The Living Insights were written by Bill Butterworth, a graduate of Florida Bible College, Dallas Theological Seminary, and Florida Atlantic University. In 2001 this guide was revised by the Pastoral Ministries Department of Insight for Living.

Editor in Chief:
Cynthia Swindoll

Study Guide Writer:
Ken Gire

Senior Editor:
Glenda Schlahta

Assistant Editor:
Karene Wells

Editor:
Christianne Varvel

Rights and Permissions:
The Meredith Agency

Text Designer:
Gary Lett

Graphic System Administrator:
Bob Haskins

ISBN 1-57972-371-3
Cover design: Michael Standlee Design

Printed in the United States of America

CONTENTS

Introduction

In a time of disappointment and disillusionment, it is refreshing to return to the Word of God and find the model of a ministry anyone could trust. In the first seven chapters of 2 Corinthians, we find ingredients that all of us admire: integrity, compassion, dedication, servanthood, realism, hope, and a half dozen other qualities worth emulating.

My desire in providing the following material is to bring our attention back to the trustworthy truths of the Scriptures from which we glean a renewed perspective regarding ministry. We can easily become jaded and cynical if our focus stays too long on ministries today where the consequences of doctrinal error and personal failure have taken their toll. It is time to lift our sights!

I invite you to take this journey with me as we walk through one scene after another that unveils the underlying secrets of an effective ministry. One warning: Be ready for a few surprises!

Chuck Swindoll

Charles R. Swindoll

Putting Truth into Action

Knowledge apart from application falls short of God's desire for His children. He wants us to apply what we learn so that we will change and grow. This Bible study guide was prepared with these goals in mind. As you go through the following pages, we hope your desire to discover biblical truth will grow as your understanding of God's Word increases and that you will be encouraged to apply what you've learned.

To assist you in your study, we've included a section called **Living Insights** at the end of each lesson. These exercises will challenge you to study further and to think of specific ways to put your discoveries into action.

There are many ways to use this guide—in personal devotions, group studies, discussions with friends and family, and Sunday School classes. And, of course, it's an ideal study aid when you're listening to its corresponding *Insight for Living* radio series.

To benefit most from this Bible study guide, we would encourage you to consider it a spiritual journal. That's why we've included space in the **Living Insights** for recording your thoughts and discoveries. We hope you'll return to those sections often for review and encouragement as you continue to grow in your walk with Christ.

Insight for Living

A Ministry Anyone Could

A Study of 2 Corinthians 1–7

Chapter 1

TELLING IT LIKE IT IS

A Survey of 2 Corinthians

Philosopher, theologian, musician, physician, philanthropist, Nobel Prize winner—are these the stars of an exceptionally brilliant graduation class? No. This is the résumé of *one* man: Albert Schweitzer.

Renowned for his philanthropic work as a mission doctor in west-central Africa for more than half of his ninety years, Schweitzer became an icon of noble, selfless service for generations. One biographer even wrote that Schweitzer practically personified "the Greek idea of the whole man—the thinker, the leader, the man of action, the scientist, the artist."[1]

But this writer also added another comment we should remember, especially as we embark on a journey with another remarkable man: the apostle Paul. The biographer wrote:

> Like all great figures in history, he becomes real not despite his frailties but because of them. . . .
>
> . . . [In observing Schweitzer,] I learned that a man does not have to be an angel to be a saint.[2]

As we'll discover in this very human letter of 2 Corinthians, God does great things with non-angelic saints. And we'll see that, as He did with Albert Schweitzer and with Paul, God can take our weaknesses and frailties and turn them into pillars of His power and praise.

1. Norman Cousins, *Albert Schweitzer's Mission* (New York, N.Y.: W. W. Norton and Co., 1985), p. 137.

2. Cousins, *Albert Schweitzer's Mission*, pp. 137, 140.

Some General Information

About Paul

Except for that of Jesus, no New Testament life looms larger than Paul's. Take a look at his impressive résumé: born in Tarsus . . .

> circumcised the eighth day, of the nation of Israel, of the tribe of Benjamin, a Hebrew of Hebrews; as to the Law, a Pharisee; as to zeal, a persecutor of the church; as to the righteousness which is in the Law, found blameless. (Phil. 3:5–6)

And all of this *before* his conversion on the Damascus road (see Acts 9:1–31). God used that road to strike Paul down by blinding him so he could lift him to incredible heights—as an apostle, evangelist, pastor, missionary, and, finally, martyr. No one was more committed to the cause of Christ than Saint Paul.

A saint? Without question. But an angel? No. Not according to his own testimony: "I am the least of the apostles . . . the very least of all saints . . . foremost of all [sinners]" (1 Cor. 15:9; Eph. 3:8; 1 Tim. 1:15).

About 2 Corinthians

Aside from his résumé, Paul penned thirteen New Testament letters. He traveled extensively, plowing new mission fields and planting a number of churches in the once-fallow Roman Empire. The letters he wrote grew out of his travels and set forth the basic theology of the Christian faith.

Second Corinthians, however, is different from Paul's other letters. It opens wide the windows of his personal life and struggles, showing him at his most transparent. Chapter 1 gives us a sample of this self-disclosure:

> We do not want you to be unaware, brethren, of our affliction which came to us in Asia, that we were burdened excessively, beyond our strength, so that we despaired even of life; indeed, we had the sentence of death within ourselves so that we would not trust in ourselves, but in God who raises the dead. (vv. 8–9)

In 4:8–11, he shared more of his struggles:

> We are afflicted in every way, but not crushed; perplexed, but not despairing; persecuted, but not forsaken; struck down, but not destroyed; always carrying about in the body the dying of Jesus, so that the life of Jesus also may be manifested in our body. For we who live are constantly being delivered over to death for Jesus' sake, so that the life of Jesus also may be manifested in our mortal flesh.

The Greek word for *perplexed* in verse 8 means "without a way." That's how Paul felt. His life looked like a confusing array of crossroads and intersections and flashing red, green, and yellow lights.

Yet because of God's grace, Paul was never utterly lost or without hope. Christ's life always preserved him, and Jesus is ready and willing to do the same for us.

Some Biblical Observations

Paul's second letter to the Corinthians is also more emotional and less structured than any of his other letters. His first letter to this group had not been well received. In fact, they disliked what he had written so much that they began attacking his authority to teach. As he wrote the second letter, a faction of Judaizers were still attempting to undermine his ministry to the Corinthians. And it was in response to that situation that he wrote.

Second Corinthians has basically three sections, though it is rife with theologically rich digressions. The first section (chaps. 1–7) finds Paul defending his conduct and his unique ministry as an apostle. The second section (chaps. 8–9) reveals him urging the Corinthians to finish readying their collection for the needy saints in Jerusalem. And the third section (chaps. 10–13) details his validation of his apostolic authority.[3]

Throughout these sections, however, we see that 2 Corinthians provides a well-stocked cupboard of food for thought. Let's bring a few of its principles down from the shelf and take a cursory look at the labels.

3. See the Bible study guide *God's Masterwork: A Concerto in Sixty-Six Movements*, vol. 4, written by Gary Matlack, Bryce Klabunde, and Wendy Peterson, from the Bible-teaching ministry of Charles R. Swindoll (Anaheim, Calif.: Insight for Living, 1997), pp. 77–85.

Great people are not immune to difficult times. Even though Paul was a great man with a great ministry, even though God's hand was obviously on his life, and even though his ministry was centered in God's perfect will, life was difficult for him.

Hard times bring tensions that are easily interpreted as unfair contradictions. Paul's driving desire was that his life would blossom as a fragrant aroma of Christ, regardless of how rocky the soil of his circumstances:

> Giving no cause for offense in anything, so that the ministry will not be discredited, but in everything commending ourselves as servants of God, in much endurance, in afflictions, in hardships, in distresses, in beatings, in imprisonments, in tumults, in labors, in sleeplessness, in hunger, in purity, in knowledge, in patience, in kindness, in the Holy Spirit, in genuine love, in the word of truth, in the power of God; by the weapons of righteousness for the right hand and the left, by glory and dishonor, by evil report and good report; regarded as deceivers and yet true; as unknown yet well-known, as dying yet behold, we live; as punished yet not put to death, as sorrowful yet always rejoicing, as poor yet making many rich, as having nothing yet possessing all things. (6:3–10)

In 11:23–27, Paul presented yet another not-so-inviting travel brochure of the Christian life:

> Are they servants of Christ?—I speak as if insane—I more so; in far more labors, in far more imprisonments, beaten times without number, often in danger of death. Five times I received from the Jews thirty-nine lashes. Three times I was beaten with rods, once I was stoned, three times I was shipwrecked, a night and a day I have spent in the deep. I have been on frequent journeys, in dangers from rivers, dangers from robbers, dangers from my countrymen, dangers from the Gentiles, dangers in the city, dangers in the wilderness, dangers on the sea, dangers among false brethren; I have been in labor and hardship, through many sleepless nights, in hunger and thirst, often without food, in cold and exposure.

Where did we ever get the idea that Christianity is a tidy, tranquil, white-picket-fence, suburban-dream kind of life? Not from Jesus. Not from Paul. A life lived by faith comes at a cost, and God has a great purpose in that cost that we don't want to miss.

Such tensions are needed reminders of our own weaknesses, forcing us to draw upon God's power. God took Paul from the darkest of valleys to the brightest of mountaintops—from prison up to Paradise (compare 11:23 with 12:1–4). But after giving Paul a heavenly revelation, God gave the apostle a humbling reminder:

> Because of the surpassing greatness of the revelations, for this reason, to keep me from exalting myself, there was given me a thorn in the flesh,[4] a messenger of Satan to torment me—to keep me from exalting myself! (12:7)

In spite of fervent, repeated prayers that this thorn be taken away (v. 8), it remained in Paul's flesh like a string tied around his finger, reminding him of an all-important truth:

> And He has said to me, "My grace is sufficient for you, for power is perfected in weakness." Most gladly, therefore, I will rather boast about my weaknesses, so that the power of Christ may dwell in me. Therefore I am well content with weaknesses, with insults, with distresses, with persecutions, with difficulties, for Christ's sake; for when I am weak, then I am strong. (vv. 9–10)

Like Paul, Scottish minister George Matheson had his own thorn in the flesh. Born in Glasgow in 1842, Matheson endured eye trouble all of his childhood. By the time he went into the ministry, he was blind. Yet for forty years he preached all across Scotland. And he wrote the words to the beautiful hymn "O Love That Will Not Let Me Go." His journal, *Thoughts for Life's Journey*,

4. Paul's "thorn in the flesh" has been the subject of much debate. Tertullian thought it was a pain in the ear or head. Chrysostom thought it was troublesome adversaries, such as Hymenaeus and Alexander. Other suggestions range from epilepsy to ophthalmia to malaria to attacks of depression. Paul, however, did not provide enough of a description to pinpoint the malady. For a further discussions, see Philip E. Hughes, *Commentary on the Second Epistle to the Corinthians* (Grand Rapids, Mich.: William B. Eerdmans Publishing Co., 1962), pp. 442–48.

tells of the lessons he learned:

> My soul, reject not the place of thy prostration! It has ever been the robing room for royalty. Ask the great ones of the past what has been the spot of their prosperity; they will say, "It was the cold ground on which I once was lying." Ask Abraham; he will point you to the sacrifice of Moriah. Ask Joseph; he will direct you to his dungeon. Ask Moses; he will date his fortune from his danger in the Nile. Ask Ruth; she will bid you build her monument in the field of her toil. Ask David; he will tell you that his songs came from the night. Ask Job; he will remind you that God answered him out of the whirlwind. Ask Peter; he will extol his submission in the sea. Ask John; he will give the palm to Patmos. Ask Paul; he will attribute his inspiration to the light that struck him blind. Ask one more—the Son of Man. Ask Him whence has come His rule over the world. He will answer, "From the cold ground on which I was lying—the Gethsemane ground; I received my sceptre there."[5]

You see, God's power is perfected in weakness. Not in degrees or in diplomas. Not in accomplishments or in accolades. Not in wealth or in wisdom. But in weakness. It is the leg that limps that leans on something other than itself for support. And so God may touch our leg so we might learn to lean on Him.

Humanity plus difficulty brings humility and maturity, not inferiority. We live in a time when weakness is despised. Even "average" isn't good enough anymore. We work insane numbers of hours trying to be superstars at work; we spend more than we can afford to drive the latest cars and wear the latest fashions; we agonize over the slightest bulge or merest blemish in our appearance. Being responsible, reliable, and presentable is no longer enough. If we can't shine in every area, we feel inferior and inadequate and resolve to try all the harder.

But Paul's attitude toward weakness—even his own—was completely different:

> Therefore I am well content with weaknesses, with

5. George Matheson, as quoted by V. Raymond Edman in *The Disciplines of Life* (Minneapolis, Minn.: World Wide Publications, 1948), p. 126.

> insults, with distresses, with persecutions, with difficulties, for Christ's sake; for when I am weak, then I am strong. (12:10)

The Christian life is a life of paradox. In weakness, we are strong. Giving, we receive. Losing, we find. Dying, we live. Consider some of the paradoxes found in 2 Corinthians that we will study in this series:

- Brokenness gives wholeness to our ministry
- Meekness brings strength into our lives
- Weakness puts power on display

Some Practical Suggestions

Jesus has been the Word of God from all eternity. But only when the Word was incarnate in the flesh could we see and touch the truth. Here are three suggestions to help you incorporate the truths of 2 Corinthians into your life so others may see and touch the truth of God:

1. Don't hide your humanity; it is directly linked to authenticity.
2. Don't deny your weaknesses and inadequacies; they open doors to God's strength.
3. Don't hesitate to call for help; your hope is in the Lord.

Living Insights

Any letter makes more sense if we know the person who wrote it. Before we delve into Paul's second letter to the Corinthians, let's get better acquainted with its author. His biography is found in Acts 9:1–31; 13. Spend some time reading through this brief account of his life, and then answer the following questions.

God told Ananias that Paul was "a chosen instrument of Mine, to bear My name before the Gentiles and kings and the sons of Israel" (Acts 9:15). Why do you think God chose Paul for this task?

____

____

Describe what you see of Paul's personality in these chapters. Include both strengths and weaknesses.

God also told Ananias that He would "show [Paul] how much he must suffer for My name's sake" (9:16). What evidence do you see that God followed through on His word? How did Paul respond to his suffering?

In this chapter, we listed the main themes Paul addressed in 2 Corinthians. From his biography, why do you think he was uniquely qualified to address these subjects?

- *Great people are not immune to difficult times.*

- *Hard times bring tensions that are easily interpreted as unfair contradictions.*

- *Such tensions are needed reminders of our own weaknesses, forcing us to draw upon God's power.*

- *Humanity plus difficulty brings humility and maturity, not inferiority.*

2 Corinthians: A Man and His Ministry

Writer: Paul
Date: A.D. 54–55
Style: Personal, Bold, Defensive

Uniqueness: This letter seems to be the least systematic of Paul's writing—these are the words of a man who freely expresses his feelings about himself and his ministry.

Introduction and Salutation	**Crucial Concerns**	**Grace Giving**	**Apostolic Authority**	Conclusion and Farewell
	Suffering and God's Sufficiency Ministry and Our Involvement Godliness and Its Impact	Example of Macedonians Command to Corinthians	Reply to Critics Justification of Ministry False Teachers Visions, Revelations, Credentials, Warnings God's Power Perfected in Weakness	
1:1–2	1:3–7:16	8:1–9:15	10:1–13:10	13:11–14
Scope:	**Past**	**Present**	**Future**	
Issues:	Misunderstandings, Concerns, Explanations	Financial Project	Vindication of Paul's Ministry	
Tone:	Forgiving, Grateful, Bold	Confident	Defensive, Strong	
Key verses:	"For we do not preach ourselves but Christ Jesus as Lord." (4:5a)	"God loves a cheerful giver." (9:7b)	"I shall not be put to shame." (10:8b)	

Chapter 2

UNRAVELING THE MYSTERY OF SUFFERING

2 Corinthians 1:1–11

Sunlight streams through stained glass windows and gleams on the wood of the padded pews. The pastor preaches a heartfelt sermon, the worshipers are glad to be together, and the choir sings in perfect harmony:

> Come, ye disconsolate, where'er ye languish;
> Come to the Mercyseat, fervently kneel.
> Here bring your wounded hearts, here tell your
> anguish;
> Earth has no sorrow that Heav'n cannot heal.[1]

It's a picture-perfect Sunday morning. But a discordant note twangs in the hearts of those who suffer. They want to believe that heaven can heal their sorrow. But illness, marital struggles, worry over children or money . . . these things have their souls tied in knots, and sometimes it feels like there are more questions than answers.

"*Why*, God? Why this? Why me? Why now?"

One thing weaves us all together into the same tapestry—suffering. From our earthly perspective, all we see is the back of the canvas, and life often looks like nothing more than snarled threads and missed stitches. We know suffering is inevitable, but in the midst of it we long to see some rhyme or reason, some purposeful pattern, a design in the making.

There *is* a pattern, and that's what this chapter is about . . . making sense of suffering.

Suffering: Unraveling Its Mystery

The Bible gives us a glimpse of the heavenward side of that tapestry in the first eleven verses of 2 Corinthians. This passage

1. Thomas Moore, "Come, Ye Disconsolate," *The Lutheran Hymnal* (St. Louis, Mo.: Concordia Publishing House, 1941), no. 531.

faces the mystery of suffering head-on and begins to untangle it, strand by strand.

Warm Words of Introduction

Written by a man whose authority had often been undermined, 2 Corinthians begins by verifying Paul's credentials:

> Paul, an apostle of Christ Jesus by the will of God, and Timothy our brother, to the church of God which is at Corinth with all the saints who are throughout Achaia. (1:1)

Paul called himself "an apostle of Christ Jesus." The Greek word *apostolos* literally means "one sent forth." It was used to describe that unique first-century individual who was gifted with the miraculous ability to speak as an oracle of God. There were only twelve apostles in the technical sense of the word—the eleven disciples plus Matthias, Judas' replacement.

Paul was an apostle, not because he inherited the role, not because he was selected by the people or appointed by some commission, and not because he appointed himself. He was an apostle "by the will of God." In contrast, Paul described Timothy affectionately as a brother. The young pastor was not an apostle but rather an apostolic delegate.

The letter is addressed to the church at Corinth and was meant to be forwarded from that commercial center to the concentric circle of believers in the region of Achaia.[2]

With the formalities aside, Paul greeted them warmly:

> Grace to you and peace from God our Father and the Lord Jesus Christ. (v. 2)

Wise Words of Explanation

Since so much of his letter will focus on pain, suffering, and heartache, it's not surprising that Paul began by explaining some of the reasons we experience trials:

> Blessed be the God and Father of our Lord Jesus Christ, the Father of mercies and God of all comfort,

2. Achaia was the Roman province comprising all the territory of Greece south of Macedonia. Presumably, copies of the letter would be made at Corinth and then circulated throughout the province.

> who comforts us in all our affliction so that we will be able to comfort those who are in any affliction with the comfort with which we ourselves are comforted by God. (vv. 3–4)

The word *comfort* almost leaps off the page. It is key to Paul's explanation. In these verses and the three that follow, the same root word is used ten times. It comes from the Greek word *paraklētos*, which is formed from the prefix *para*, meaning "alongside," and the root *kaleō*, meaning "to call." Comfort is given by someone called alongside to help—like a nurse called to a patient's bedside. It's the same word John 14:16 uses for the Holy Spirit: "I will ask the Father, and He will give you another Helper [Comforter], that He may be with you forever."

When tragedy strikes, collapsing our life like a house of cards, comfort is what we need most. We need someone to come alongside and put an arm around us, to be there, to listen, to help. We need the *Paraklētos*, the Father of mercies and the God of all comfort. And He promises us His presence.

We also need to know our suffering has some purpose. In Romans 8:28, Paul assured us that for those who love God, He causes "all things to work together for good." In 2 Corinthians 1:4–11, Paul told us three of the ways that suffering brings about good in our lives. The first is found in verse 4:

> who comforts us in all our affliction so that we will be able to comfort those who are in any affliction with the comfort with which we ourselves are comforted by God.

Suffering prepares us to comfort others. It's a chain reaction: when we go through suffering, God comforts us. And when His comfort has done its work in our lives, then we, in turn, can comfort others in similar situations. A perfect example of this is Joni Eareckson Tada. God has comforted her in her paralysis, and she, in turn, has comforted thousands of other people with physical disabilities.

Someone who has suffered the shattering effects of a divorce is the best person to comfort a divorcée. The parent who has lost a child can best comfort another grieving parent. The businessman who once was bankrupt can best comfort another person in the throes of financial disaster. One reason God allows suffering is so we might have a well of experiences deep enough from which to draw compassion and counsel for others:

> For just as the sufferings of Christ are ours in abundance, so also our comfort is abundant through Christ. (v. 5)

God's salve is dispensed in proportion to the extent of our wounds. And that salve is stored in us so at the appropriate time we might dispense it to others:

> But if we are afflicted, it is for your comfort and salvation; or if we are comforted, it is for your comfort, which is effective in the patient enduring of the same sufferings which we also suffer; and our hope for you is firmly grounded, knowing that as you are sharers of our sufferings, so also you are sharers of our comfort. (vv. 6–7)

Lest we think Paul's advice is only theoretical, he recounted a dark chapter in his life to show us that these principles come straight from the textbook of real life:

> For we do not want you to be unaware, brethren, of our affliction which came to us in Asia, that we were burdened excessively, beyond our strength, so that we despaired even of life. (v. 8)

We don't know what "affliction" Paul faced in Asia, but it was obviously extreme. The Greek word for *despaired* is *exaporeō*, and it implies "the total unavailability of an exit."[3] Apparently, Paul viewed himself as being on the brink of death. But while teetering on that brink, he discovered a second purpose in suffering found in verse 9:

> indeed, we had the sentence of death within ourselves so that we would not trust in ourselves, but in God who raises the dead.

Suffering keeps us from trusting in ourselves. Intense suffering is designed to remind us of our utter helplessness—for it is when we

3. See Murray J. Harris, "2 Corinthians," in *The Expositor's Bible Commentary*, gen. ed. Frank E. Gaebelein (Grand Rapids, Mich.: Zondervan Publishing House, Regency Reference Library, 1976), vol. 10, p. 321.

are most helpless that we are most dependent. Proverbs 3:5–6 tells us:

> Trust in the Lord with all your heart
> And do not lean on your own understanding.
> In all your ways acknowledge Him,
> And He will make your paths straight.

The world's advice, however, is diametrically opposed to this wisdom. We're encouraged to "stand tall" and urged to believe we can handle anything. The truth is, there are many things in life that knock us flat, any number of situations we *can't* handle. Our own hearts can deceive us, and our brains are capable of error. But when things are running smoothly, it's easy to forget our weaknesses. Suffering reorients us to the truth.

Yet thankfully, suffering is not God's final plan for His children. Through the impassioned pen of the weeping prophet, Jeremiah—who was also well acquainted with grief—God gave us one of the grandest promises in the Bible:

> "'For I know the plans that I have for you,' declares the Lord, "plans for welfare and not for calamity to give you a future and a hope.'" (Jer. 29:11)

You may think there's no rhyme or reason to the doggerel verse of pain you're experiencing. But in God's eyes, your pain is just the first line of a poem He is making.

Paul concluded his introduction with a thank-you note that provides the third purpose in suffering:

> who delivered us from so great a peril of death, and will deliver us, He on whom we have set our hope. And He will yet deliver us, you also joining in helping us through your prayers, so that thanks may be given by many persons on our behalf for the favor bestowed on us through the prayers of many. (2 Cor. 1:10–11)

Suffering teaches us to give thanks in everything. In *everything?* Even suffering? Even *exaporeō*—those back-against-the-wall situations that promise nothing more than certain doom?

Even in those. Why? Because even in those circumstances, God is prodding you toward His perfect plan, toward the future He has prepared for you.

Suffering: Handling Its Perplexities

> Suffering prepares us to comfort others.
> Suffering keeps us from trusting in ourselves.
> Suffering teaches us to give thanks in everything.

Sounds good, doesn't it? As long as you're not in the midst of a trial! How can we take these principles off the page and put them into our lives? The next time suffering shows up in your life, try implementing these three suggestions:

1. Instead of focusing only on yourself now, think of how you can help others later. This will sound a note of hope.

2. Rather than fighting, surrender; rather than resisting, release. This will produce a note of faith.

3. Although getting even seems to come more naturally, try giving thanks. This will bring a note of peace.

Hope. Faith. Peace. Hear the melody? Hear the harmony? Let Christ turn your suffering into a symphony. And where there was only the discord of instruments warming up, He will orchestrate a musical score that would make even Beethoven stand up and applaud.

Living Insights

It's easy to wax eloquent on the benefits of suffering when your life is relatively pain-free. Finding good in heartache is much more difficult when you are in the midst of it.

It may be difficult, even impossible, to see the beauty that God will bring out of your despair, at least for right now. But while you may not be able to see His plan, you can feel His comfort.

The word *comfort* appears ten times in the passage we studied in this chapter. For each time that word appears, write down one example of comfort you have experienced, either from God Himself or from someone He sent your way. And while you're at it, take comfort in remembering!

1. ____

____

2. ____

____

3. ____

____

4. ____

____

5. ____

____

6. ____

____

7. ____

____

8. ____

____

9. ____

____

10. ____

____

Chapter 3

IN DEFENSE OF INTEGRITY

2 Corinthians 1:12–2:4

One of the smallest muscles in the human body is also the most destructive. In seconds it can cut and slash, leaving its victim in emotional shreds. This muscle is the tongue. Concerning it, Washington Irving wrote:

> A sharp tongue is the only edge tool that grows keener with common use.[1]

The tongue can ruin a reputation, malign a motive, and destroy one's dignity. This lethal weapon may be wielded publicly without shame. But more often it is a dagger cloaked in stealth, stabbing its victim in the back.

Surprisingly, the fingerprints on this dagger often do not point to a hardened criminal but to some haloed saint who only minutes before might have sung the sweetest song, uttered the most beautiful prayer, or spoken the most encouraging words.

James mentioned this incongruity in the third chapter of his book:

> No one can tame the tongue; it is a restless evil and full of deadly poison. With it we bless our Lord and Father, and with it we curse men, who have been made in the likeness of God; from the same mouth come both blessing and cursing. My brethren, these things ought not to be this way. (vv. 8–10)

If you've felt the thrust of the dagger between your shoulder blades, you're not alone. David also knew the piercing pain of an assassinated character, and his cry for vindication is recorded in Psalm 7:

> O Lord my God, in You I have taken refuge;
> Save me from all those who pursue me, and deliver me,
> Or he will tear my soul like a lion,
> Dragging me away, while there is none to deliver.

1. *Bartlett's Familiar Quotations*, 14th ed., rev. and enl., ed. Emily Morison Beck (Boston, Mass.: Little, Brown and Co., 1968), p. 550.

O Lord my God, if I have done this,
If there is injustice in my hands,
If I have rewarded evil to my friend,
Or have plundered him who without cause was my
adversary,
Let the enemy pursue my soul and overtake it;
And let him trample my life down to the ground
And lay my glory in the dust. Selah.
Arise, O Lord, in Your anger;
Lift up Yourself against the rage of my adversaries,
And arouse Yourself for me; You have appointed
judgment.
Let the assembly of the peoples encompass You,
And over them return on high.
The Lord judges the peoples;
Vindicate me, O Lord, according to my righteousness and my integrity that is in me. (vv. 1–8)

In the final analysis, all we have is our reputation. You can take away my business, my money, and my possessions. But take a stab at my integrity and you've attacked the very core of my life. That's what was so precious to David, and that is why he prayed so fervently:

Vindicate me, O Lord, for I have walked in my
integrity,
And I have trusted in the Lord without wavering.
Examine me, O Lord, and try me;
Test my mind and my heart.
For Your lovingkindness is before my eyes,
And I have walked in Your truth. . . .
But as for me, I shall walk in my integrity;
Redeem me, and be gracious to me. (Ps. 26:1–3, 11)

The Pain of Enduring False Accusation

We all chanted it when we were young: "Sticks and stones may break my bones, but words will never hurt me." Nevertheless, words do hurt. Those hard, verbal attacks inflict wounds as damaging as any bodily ones.

Among the many trials we face, few are more devastating than statements made against us. They may be made against our *conduct*—things we didn't do; against our *words*—things we didn't say; or against our *motives*—things we didn't mean. Paul experienced all three, and in 2 Corinthians 1, we see his rebuttal.

In Defense of True Character

Most of us respond to false accusations in one of two ways. We either bite our tongues and hope the matter will blow over or we explode in outrage. Both are understandable, but neither is productive. The first response leaves the lie unanswered; the second only compounds the problem. Paul showed us a better way to respond—calmly, but with the truth.

Carnal Conduct

Verse 12 implies that Paul's conduct and sincerity had been called into question. Paul refuted the accusation with directness and certainty:

> For our proud confidence is this: the testimony of our conscience, that in holiness and godly sincerity, not in fleshly wisdom but in the grace of God, we have conducted ourselves in the world, and especially toward you.

How many of us could claim that we're consistently holy and sincere? Most of us would be reluctant to allow an in-depth probe of our lives. But Paul opened up his life and his writings for examination without fear:

> For we write nothing else to you than what you read and understand, and I hope you will understand until the end; just as you also partially did understand us, that we are your reason to be proud as you also are ours, in the day of our Lord Jesus. (vv. 13–14)

Fickle Vacillation

Evidently, rumors were being spread that Paul made promises he didn't keep. It was true that Paul had not come to visit the Corinthians as he had intended. In verses 15–16, he admitted:

> In this confidence I intended at first to come to you, so that you might twice receive a blessing; that is, to pass your way into Macedonia, and again from

> Macedonia to come to you, and by you to be helped on my journey to Judea.

But we can also see the original wording of Paul's plan in 1 Corinthians 16:5–7, and even a cursory reading shows that his suggested visit came with plenty of qualifications:

> But I will come to you after I go through Macedonia, for I am going through Macedonia; and perhaps I will stay with you, or even spend the winter, so that you may send me on my way wherever I may go. For I do not wish to see you now just in passing; for I hope to remain with you for some time, if the Lord permits.

The Corinthians mistook Paul's full intentions for a firm promise. And when he didn't come, they concluded, "If you can't trust a man to keep a promise, how can you respect his authority as an apostle?"

In self-defense, Paul argued that his change in plans was not capricious. He had every intention of visiting them, but circumstances postponed his travel plans:

> I was not vacillating when I intended to do this, was I? Or what I purpose, do I purpose according to the flesh, so that with me there will be yes, yes and no, no at the same time?[2] But as God is faithful, our word to you is not yes and no. For the Son of God, Christ Jesus, who was preached among you by us—by me and Silvanus and Timothy—was not yes and no, but is yes in Him. For as many as are the promises of God, in Him they are yes; therefore also through Him is our Amen to the glory of God through us. Now He who establishes us with you in Christ and anointed us is God, who also sealed[3] us and gave us the Spirit in our hearts as a pledge. (2 Cor. 1:17–22)

2. In the original Greek, this question is introduced by the negative word *mēti*, which expects no for an answer.

3. The Greek word is *sphragizō*. The middle voice of the verb carries the sense that the Holy Spirit sealed us for Himself. "The seal, given and preserved intact, was proof that a document had not been falsified, or goods tampered with in transit. It was also a mark of ownership; and the Christian, sealed . . . with the Spirit, was both visibly marked out as God's property, and secured ready to meet examination at the day of judgement." C. K. Barrett, *A Commentary on the Second Epistle to the Corinthians* (New York, N.Y.: Harper and Row, Publishers, 1973), p. 79.

In fact, the reason Paul didn't go to Corinth was that he wanted to spare them sorrow:

> But I call God as witness to my soul, that to spare you I did not come again to Corinth. . . .
>
> But I determined this for my own sake, that I would not come to you in sorrow again. For if I cause you sorrow, who then makes me glad but the one whom I made sorrowful? This is the very thing I wrote you, so that when I came, I would not have sorrow from those who ought to make me rejoice; having confidence in you all that my joy would be the joy of you all. For out of much affliction and anguish of heart I wrote to you with many tears; not so that you would be made sorrowful, but that you might know the love which I have especially for you. (1:23; 2:1–4)

Apparently, Paul had written them an additional letter after 1 Corinthians. And apparently, too, it was a blistering one, perhaps relating to the incestuous relationship denounced in 1 Corinthians 5:1–8. On the heels of that letter, Paul didn't want his arrival to stir up the sorrow his letter had created. He wanted to wait until the matter was resolved and the church was joyful again. His words are those of a loving shepherd, not a self-serving tyrant.

Dominating Dictator

From 2 Corinthians 1:24, we can infer that the Corinthians were also charging Paul with wanting to throw his spiritual weight around, trying to be some sort of guru for people to coweringly follow:

> Not that we lord it over your faith, but are workers with you for your joy; for in your faith you are standing firm.

You'd have to want power pretty badly to endure the things Paul went through in order to spread the gospel (see 11:23–27)! Instead, Paul viewed himself as a fellow worker (1:24) and a servant (4:5).

Servanthood is a rare quality today mainly because there are so few examples of it. In the church, pastors, teachers, elders, and deacons often lord their leadership position over the flock. In the workplace, employers often lord it over their employees. In the home, husbands often lord it over their wives, and parents often lord it over their children. Maybe the problem stems from not having our eyes on the ultimate Servant—Jesus, who came not to be served but to serve (Mark 10:45).

How about you? Do you lord it over others? Or do you look to the Lord and use Him as your example for leadership?

When You Stand Accused

Paul was not the first to face false accusations, and we all know he wasn't the last. Sooner or later, all of us will find ourselves on the wrong end of a critical tongue. But when we do, there are some principles that will help us fend off its effects.

There are times when defending one's integrity calls for strong action. When you know who is starting the gossip, it's time for confrontation. Don't talk with a lot of other people—just go directly to the person doing the damage. But keep your cool! Losing your temper will only fuel the fire.

There are times when the best response is silence. In a few cases, silence may be the best defense: if you don't know who the accuser is; if the accuser is unavailable; or if the more you defend yourself, the more you appear guilty. Instead of speaking out, go immediately to God, plead for vindication, and then step out of the way and let Him fight the battle (see Ps. 26).

Whether with assertiveness or silence, never take revenge. Whichever approach you use, leave the paybacks out of it. Remember, "Vengeance is Mine," said the Lord (Deut. 32:35). If justice is to be meted out, let God be the one to handle it.

Living Insights

Before we can defend integrity, we need to make sure we know what it is and whether or not we have it. Psalm 15 is an excellent resource on the subject. Read it through, and then list the traits integrity encompasses.

____

____

____

____

If someone were to really examine your life, how "holy and sincere" would you appear? Look at your list again. Which of those traits do you feel confident are evidenced in your life? Which do you feel are weaker areas?

____

____

____

____

Ask God to strengthen your "integrity image" so that you can claim with Paul that your life bears up to examination.

Chapter 4

When Forgiveness Really Means Probation

2 Corinthians 2:5–11

There is nothing quite as liberating as being forgiven. To have wronged someone and regretted it, to have felt the rift it created, to have wished back those words or those deeds . . . and then to be pardoned—what a great feeling of relief, of gratitude! The slate is wiped clean; the relationship is restored. Those three little words, "I forgive you," are almost as dear to us as the words "I love you."

As long as they're said honestly, that is. Sometimes people say, "I forgive you," when what they really mean is, "You're on probation." *Webster's* says that *probation* is "the subjection of an individual to a period of testing and trial to ascertain fitness." It's "freedom . . . under supervision."[1] Instead of leaving you feeling liberated, it makes you feel unsettled, watched, distrusted.

Some circumstances do call for caution: when we're not sure repentance is genuine . . . when the sentiment is real, but restitution is lagging . . . when steps haven't been taken to prevent recurrence. But when forgiveness *is* called for, it should be complete, no holds barred, no grudge held in reserve for future ammunition.

That statement begs a question: When *is* forgiveness called for? The Corinthians wrestled with the same issue. Let's first look at how Jesus addressed the issue, then we'll see how Paul applied Jesus' teaching in Corinth.

Christ's Guidelines on Forgiveness

Matthew's gospel contains a magnificent section on the subject of forgiveness in 18:21–35. Here Jesus answered three questions: How often should I forgive someone? Why not stop at a certain limit? What if I choose not to do as You have said?

1. *Merriam-Webster's Collegiate Dictionary*, 10th ed., see "probation."

How Often?

In verse 21, Peter asked:

> "Lord, how often shall my brother sin against me and I forgive him? Up to seven times?"

Haven't we all felt like asking the same thing? Peter most likely thought he was being pretty generous, since the religious leaders of his day put the limit at three. But Jesus' answer surprised him:

> "I do not say to you, up to seven times, but up to seventy times seven." (v. 22)

Jesus didn't mean that we should literally forgive someone 490 times and then let them have it on the 491st. He was saying there *isn't* a limit. The number is *infinity*.

Why Not?

Jesus anticipated Peter's next question and answered it before it was asked: "Why not put a limit on forgiveness?" The story Jesus told next makes it clear (see vv. 23–35). It revolves around a king whose slave owed him an astronomical sum, equivalent to ten million dollars. Since the slave couldn't repay the money, he and his family were sentenced to be sold. But the slave fell on his face and begged for more time. The response of the king was extravagantly merciful:

> "And the lord of that slave felt compassion and released him and forgave him the debt." (v. 27)

By comparison, our Lord has forgiven us an infinite debt—our sin. That is why we should forgive others an infinite amount. As Paul said in Ephesians 4:32, we are to be "forgiving each other, just as God in Christ also has forgiven you." To do anything less for another is a gross act of hypocrisy . . . as we see in the next part of the story.

The pardoned slave left the king's presence and met one of his fellow slaves who owed him a small amount of money. Rather than forgiving as he had been forgiven, the slave showed no mercy, insisting on immediate compensation. When the man couldn't pay, the slave had the man thrown into prison. The king got wind of what had happened and confronted the slave:

> "Then summoning him, his lord said to him, 'You

> wicked slave, I forgave you all that debt because you pleaded with me. Should you not also have had mercy on your fellow slave, in the same way that I had mercy on you?'" (Matt. 18:32–33)

What If?

For people like us who know our weaknesses, the next questions are obvious: "What if we don't forgive? What if probation sounds like a better idea?" Jesus' parable answers that one as well:

> "And his lord, moved with anger, handed him over to the torturers until he should repay all that was owed him. My heavenly Father will also do the same to you, if each of you does not forgive his brother from your heart." (vv. 34–35)

Ray Stedman expressed how "torture" characterizes our experience when we choose not to forgive:

> It is an accurate description of gnawing resentment and bitterness, the awful fall of hate or envy. We feel strongly this separation from another and every time we think of them we feel within the acid of resentment and hate eating away at our peace and calmness.[2]

The Corinthians' Failure to Forgive

Stedman's words illustrate what the Corinthians were feeling toward one of their brothers in Christ when they received Paul's letter.

The Problem

To understand the problem, we need to look back to 1 Corinthians 5, where Paul confronted this group about a sin they had been condoning. Apparently, one of their members was having an incestuous relationship with his stepmother (v. 1). This scandal would have shocked the Gentile community, but it hardly raised an eyebrow in the church. In fact, the church was even proud about it, apparently feeling very progressive and sophisticated in their distorted expression of Christian liberty and grace (v. 2). In no

2. Ray C. Stedman, "Breaking the Resentment Barrier," sermon delivered to Peninsula Bible Church, Palo Alto, California, *Treasures of the Parable Series*, message 11, July 13, 1969, p. 6.

uncertain terms, Paul told them that just as the Jews cleaned out the leaven from their houses during Passover (vv. 6–7), so the Corinthians must remove the immoral man from their midst (vv. 11–13).

The Punishment

Somewhere between Paul's first and second letters to the Corinthians, the church must have brought the gavel down hard on this man (2 Cor. 2:6–7). The incident isn't mentioned specifically, but it seems likely that this is what Paul had in mind when he said:

> But if any has caused sorrow, he has caused sorrow not to me, but in some degree—in order not to say too much—to all of you. Sufficient for such a one is this punishment which was inflicted by the majority. (vv. 5–6)

The Pardon

Apparently, the man had been disciplined by the church and had repented. But instead of welcoming him back with open arms, the congregation held him at arm's length. Instead of forgiving him, they put him on probation. The pendulum had swung too far, and Paul attempted to bring it back to center:

> So that on the contrary you should rather forgive and comfort him, otherwise such a one might be overwhelmed by excessive sorrow. Wherefore I urge you to reaffirm your love for him. For to this end also I wrote, so that I might put you to the test, whether you are obedient in all things. (vv. 7–9)

The man no longer needed discipline; he needed forgiveness. Notice the process: punishment (v. 6), which leads to repentance; forgiveness (v. 7a), which prevents despair; comfort (v. 7b), which rebuilds esteem and dignity; and reaffirmation of love (v. 8), which gives purpose and direction to life within the community.

With his next words, Paul went on to tell the Corinthians why forgiveness is so important:

> But one whom you forgive anything, I forgive also; for indeed what I have forgiven, if I have forgiven anything, I did it for your sakes in the presence of Christ, so that no advantage would be taken of us

> by Satan, for we are not ignorant of his schemes. (vv. 10–11)

This is one of the strongest warnings in all of Paul's letters. The phrase "by Satan" suggests that Satan takes a hands-on approach when we refuse to forgive. Not only does he get his way when a brother or sister sins, but he gets his way again when that person repents, and we remain turned away from them. He gets his way in our hearts, benefiting not only from the sinner's fall but also from our failure to forgive.

The word *scheme* in verse 11 comes from the Greek word for "the mind." Satan's schemes are mind games in which he distorts our thinking. In the case of the Corinthians, he deceived them into thinking that church discipline is all judgment and no grace. But the goal of discipline is not removal; it's restoration and reconciliation. When we lose sight of that, we go too far.

The parable of the prodigal son illustrates how we should respond to the repentant believer who wants to return to the fellowship of the church. Remember what the father said when the wayward son came to his senses and returned home?

"Okay, stay in your room for the next three months, and remember, I'll be watching you."

Of course not. You know the story:

> "While he was still a long way off, his father saw him and felt compassion for him, and ran and embraced him and kissed him. . . . The father said to his slaves, 'Quickly bring out the best robe and put it on him, and put a ring on his hand and sandals on his feet; and bring the fattened calf, kill it, and let us eat and celebrate; for this son of mine was . . . lost and has been found.'" (Luke 15:20b, 22–24)

That's how it's supposed to be. When there's repentance, when the sinner comes home, we ought to have a party! Our forgiveness should be as swift as our discipline.

Christian Principles for Today

We've watched three stories unfold. We've seen a man who was forgiven much refuse to forgive another man even a little. We've seen a repentant sinner in need of restoration. And we've seen a father fling his arms around a son who returned home. From these three stories, we can take three principles to heart.

First, *true repentance calls for immediate and full forgiveness.* When sinners truly see the error of their ways, they are likely to come back to the fold with hat in hand, as the prodigal son did (see Luke 15:18–19). The sense of shame and unworthiness can be almost overwhelming. The prodigal son wanted only to come back as his father's slave, and he rehearsed his speech all the way home, trying to get up the nerve to present it. But his father didn't even let him get the words out (vv. 20–22). The body of Christ has no probation period for repentant sinners. True repentance—heartfelt, not a shallow imitation—calls for restoration and celebration.

Second, *full forgiveness is demonstrative, not theoretical.* It's not simply something we say; it's something we do. Remember the commands in 2 Corinthians 2:7–8? They're all action words: "forgive . . . comfort . . . reaffirm."

Third, *to hold back invites trouble from the Adversary.* When you refuse to forgive someone who has genuinely repented, that person becomes confused and unproductive, wondering, "What else must I do? How else can I prove myself? Will I ever be used again by God?" Ultimately, bitterness sets in, and Satan claims another victory.

Are you holding others in bondage who deserve to be free? Are you still keeping tally of their wrongs though they've confessed them and repented? If so, ask yourself one question: Why?

If you're the one who's fallen and is living an unproductive life, distant from your family and from God, here's some good news:

> If we confess our sins, He is faithful and righteous to forgive us our sins and to cleanse us from all unrighteousness. (1 John 1:9)

Come back to Christ, won't you? Confess the sin. Be cleansed. And let Him throw His arms around you and welcome you back.

Living Insights

Which side of the forgiveness issue are you on right now? Is there someone in your life who has wronged you, or have you wronged someone else? Describe the situation.

____

____

If someone has sinned against you, what's stopping you from forgiving them?

❑ A lack of repentance on the part of the wrongdoer

❑ An unwillingness on your part

If you are in need of forgiveness, why haven't you received it?

❑ You haven't repented or asked for forgiveness

❑ The person you sinned against is unwilling to forgive you

Is there anything you can do to help the situation move toward reconciliation, such as letting the person know how you feel, praying for God's help, or talking with a pastor or counselor?

Chapter 5

WHAT IS THAT FRAGRANCE?

2 Corinthians 2:12–17

Conversation ebbs and flows around us all day long, some of it significant, some insignificant, all of it helping us feel connected to one another. *How* connected we feel, though, depends on the level of communication we have with one another.

Years ago John Powell wrote a book called *Why Am I Afraid to Tell You Who I Am?* In it he described five levels of communication that determine the kinds of relationships we have with others.

The first level consists of *clichés*. This is what we say to strangers in an elevator or acquaintances at the grocery store. It consists of well-worn phrases with little meaning: "Nice day." "Good to see you."

The second level involves *facts and reports*. It isn't quite conversation-in-passing, but it stays on safe ground—the weather, who won the game, the nightly news. It's a pleasant exchange, but with little personal information shared.

The third level is the first to scratch below the surface. Including *opinions and judgments*, it reveals a glimpse of ourselves and how we think: "I like rainy days." "I don't care for that new coach." "The city really should do something about these potholes!" This is as deep as most conversations go.

The fourth level becomes more personal, allowing *emotions* to come out of hiding: "I'm feeling blue today" or "I'm so angry at my husband right now!" At this level, we begin to feel vulnerable, a little exposed. We generally keep this level of communication limited to our close friends.

The fifth level is called *maximum truth*. Reserved for very few relationships in our lives (if any), communication on this level speaks the truth openly, candidly, and deeply. At this level, we share our dreams and disillusionments, we confess our sins, we confront sin in others, we tell and keep secrets. It is connection in the deepest sense.[1]

Each level of communication has its place. We're uncomfortable, for instance, when a stranger on a bus bares his soul to us or when an acquaintance asks probing questions we'd rather not answer. We

1. See John Powell, *Why Am I Afraid to Tell You Who I Am?* (Niles, Ill.: Argus Communications, 1969), pp. 54–58.

need the fifth level of communication in our lives, but it should take place in a relationship where trust has developed gradually through the other levels.

In 2 Corinthians, we're allowed to eavesdrop on a "level-five" letter between Paul and his friends in Corinth. We tend to think of Paul primarily as a go-getter and theologian; his letters don't always reveal the full emotional bond he shared with his readers. But in this passage, we'll see the depth of those emotions.

Paul's Life: An Open Book

Second Corinthians is an immensely personal letter. We've seen Paul's openness since the first chapter, and Eugene Peterson's paraphrase captures it especially well:

> We don't want you in the dark, friends, about how hard it was when all this came down on us in Asia province. It was so bad we didn't think we were going to make it. We felt like we'd been sent to death row, that it was all over for us. (THE MESSAGE)

And again in chapter two:

> There was pain enough just in writing that letter, more tears than ink on the parchment. But I didn't write it to cause pain; I wrote it so you would know how much I care—oh, more than care—*love* you![2] (THE MESSAGE)

Paul was a man of passion. But his passion wasn't merely sentimental—when called for, it took the form of rebuke. Painful as he found it at times, Paul didn't hesitate to probe the lives of those he loved—as we saw when the Corinthian believers took discipline too far:

> What the majority of you agreed to as punishment is punishment enough. Now is the time to forgive this man and help him back on his feet. If all you do is pour on the guilt, you could very well drown

2. Eugene H. Peterson, *The Message: The New Testament in Contemporary English* (Colorado Springs, Colo.: NavPress, 1993), pp. 369, 371.

> him in it. My counsel now is to pour on the love.[3] (THE MESSAGE)

It is in this context of vulnerability that Paul went on to share his recent personal struggle, one he faced as he ministered at Troas.

A Personal Struggle at Troas

Troas was the northwesternmost city in Asia Minor, or Turkey, as it is known now—a long way from Ephesus, where Paul had been ministering. It was no doubt a long, hard journey, but when he arrived, he found people eager to hear his message. The door was flung wide open . . . yet Paul found himself unable to walk through it:

> Now when I came to Troas for the gospel of Christ and when a door was opened for me in the Lord, I had no rest for my spirit, not finding Titus my brother; but taking my leave of them, I went on to Macedonia. (2:12–13)

The word translated *rest* can also be interpreted "relaxing." It's the same word used in Acts 24:23 for "freedom" and in 2 Corinthians 8:13 for "ease." Despite God's work in Troas, Paul felt restless and uneasy, churning inside. He had no inner peace.

Why? He couldn't find Titus, his dear friend and brother in the Lord. Apparently, Titus was supposed to meet Paul in Troas to update him on the Corinthian situation and to help him in his ministry there, but Titus was nowhere to be found. David K. Lowery helps us understand Paul's concern:

> In addition to his apprehension about the church in Corinth, Paul was now also concerned about Titus' safety. For all Paul knew Titus might have been carrying with him a portion of the proposed Corinthian collection (cf. 2 Cor. 8:6) and fallen prey to bandits. Why else had he failed to meet Paul in Troas? . . .
>
> Despairing at his own inability to concentrate on the great potential for ministry in Troas (cf. 7:5–6) Paul said good-by to the church there and pushed on to Macedonia. The door would remain open for

3. Peterson, *The Message*, p. 371.

> him and on his return (cf. Acts 20:5–11) God used him mightily in their midst, but for the moment Paul departed, unable to rise to the occasion, no doubt feeling like a beaten man. (cf. 2 Cor. 4:9)[4]

Paul didn't linger on those difficult feelings, though. Instead, he changed the subject—from himself, defeated, to Christ, who triumphs over every circumstance.

A General Statement of Ministry

Beginning in 2:14 and continuing through 6:10, Paul discussed ministry in greater depth than he did anywhere else in the New Testament. He began this section as if peering through a magnifying glass, focusing on three essentials of effective Christ-centered ministry (2:14–17). Let's take a look at what they are.

Ministry Is Following the Leader, Not Taking the Lead

> But thanks be to God, who always leads us in triumph in Christ. (v. 14a)

Few have been called to minister who are more gifted than the apostle Paul. Few have had brighter minds, stronger determination, or greater vision. And yet this gifted man openly admitted that God was the One who led the way, not him. It wasn't even a partnership. In Paul's mind, he was merely riding the coattails of the One who is truly in charge. William Barclay helps us see the picture that was in Paul's mind when he used the word *triumph:*

> In a Triumph the procession of the victorious general marched through the streets of Rome to the capitol in the following order. First came the state officials and the senate. Then came the trumpeters. Then were carried the spoils taken from the conquered land. . . . Then came pictures of the conquered land and models of conquered citadels and ships. . . . Then there walked the captive princes, leaders, and generals in chains, shortly to be flung into prison and in all probability almost immediately to be

4. David K. Lowery, "2 Corinthians," in *The Bible Knowledge Commentary,* New Testament edition, ed. John F. Walvoord and Roy B. Zuck (Colorado Springs, Colo.: Chariot Victor Publishing, 1983), p. 559.

> executed. Then came the lictors bearing their rods, followed by the musicians with their lyres; then the priests swinging their censers with the sweet-smelling incense burning in them. After that came the general himself. He stood in a chariot drawn by four horses. . . . After him rode his family; and finally came the army wearing all their decorations and shouting *Io triumphe!* their cry of triumph.[5]

Christ, our Conqueror, leads us into battle, and He leads us in the parade of triumph. He chooses the battles, and He claims the victory. Remember, at the cross Christ undertook a battle that was not rightly His so that we might share in a triumph that is not rightly ours.

Ministry Is Emitting a Pleasing Fragrance to God, Not Being Overly Concerned with the Response of Others

> [God] manifests through us the sweet aroma of the knowledge of Him in every place. For we are a fragrance of Christ to God among those who are being saved and among those who are perishing; to the one an aroma from death to death, to the other an aroma from life to life. (vv. 14b–16a)

In the ancient processional that Barclay describes, an aroma was emitted along the way by giant jars of smoking incense carried by the priests. The smell would flow equally over those exulting in triumph and those hanging their heads in defeat. To the former, it was the sweet scent of a victorious life; to the latter, an acrid reminder of their imminent death.

Whether of life or death, the aroma emanates from Christ in us. His words, His story, His love—these are the fragrant scents we share.

Ministry Is Modeling the Truth Though Inadequate, Not Corrupting the Message While Appearing Adequate

> And who is adequate for these things? For we are not like many, peddling the word of God, but as from sincerity, but as from God, we speak in Christ in the sight of God. (vv. 16b–17)

5. William Barclay, *The Letters to the Corinthians*, rev. ed., The Daily Study Bible Series (Philadelphia, Pa.: The Westminster Press, 1975), pp. 183–84.

Peddling the word of God. The image is one of street salesmen hawking their wares, interested only in making the sale—not in serving the customer. Just as there were money changers in the temple courtyard, there will always be street salesmen in the church peddling prophetic pills . . . cure-all tonics . . . positive thinking . . . health and wealth . . . legalism and negativism. In short, peddling whatever the public is gullible enough to purchase.

Paul assured the Corinthians that he was no salesman. He represented the Lord, not himself. His adequacy was not in his persuasive words but in the authority of the One who sent him and the content of his message—Christ.

Our Lives . . . An Honest Evaluation

Now that we've looked into the open book of Paul's life, it's time to read a page or two from our own. Let's take a closer look by examining four crucial categories.

First, *are you really depending upon God?* Are you waiting on Him? Or do you take advantage of every opportunity that comes your way and plow right into it? Are you sensitive to God's leading? Remember, a need doesn't constitute a call. Nor does an open door necessarily mean you are the one to walk through it.

Second, *is your life truly triumphant in Christ?* Is your focus on Christ's conquering power? Remember, God "always leads us in triumph in Christ" (v. 14).

Third, *how's your fragrance?* Are you wearing My Sin or My Savior these days? Christ has an unmistakable fragrance, and you can smell it on someone who is genuinely Christlike. Unfortunately, there's a fragrance of the flesh that's just as obvious.

Fourth, *do you sincerely model authenticity?* Is being real one of your goals? Authenticity is coming to grips with who you are and being transparent about what your life is like beneath its polished exterior. It's painful to be real, but that's the way we impact others most deeply.[6]

6. "We wish we were better than we are, but we're not. And that realization brings shame, a desire to hide, to avoid real contact, to present to others only that part of us we think will be well received. We want to hide the rest—not because we desire to avoid offending others with our ugly side, but because we fear their rejection. We live for the purpose of self-protection, clinging to whatever brings us happiness and security. The effect is a discouraging distance between ourself and the people we long to be close to. The quality of our life diminishes." Larry Crabb, *Inside Out* (Colorado Springs, Colo.: NavPress, 1988), p. 30.

If you answered no to any of these questions, maybe your relationship with the Lord is stuck at a superficial level. Fortunately, just as God always leads in triumph, so He always leads His children into a deeper relationship with Him, always encouraging us to communicate on level five. If you want to have a deeper, more meaningful spiritual life, take some time now to pray about that. And when you pray, don't worry about making King James proud. God is pleased with your stutters if only you are sincere.

Living Insights

Let's go back to those questions at the end of the chapter and take the time to ponder our answers.

1. Are you depending on God not just for ministries to become involved in, but for the results as well? What about the circumstances of your daily life—are you depending on Him to take care of each detail and direction you take?

   Definitely Sometimes Not really

   If you shy away from relying on Him, what keeps you from drawing closer? Busyness? Forgetfulness? Maybe a disappointment in the past? How can you move past that barrier into total trust?

   ____

   ____

   ____

   ____

2. Do you see evidence of Christ's triumph in your life?

   Definitely Sometimes Not really

   What areas of your life do you need Christ to triumph over? How can you get in touch with His power?

   ____

   ____

   ____

   ____

3. How's your fragrance before the Lord?

   Sweet   Bland   Offensive

   Which areas of your life do you think most please God? Which need a little more zest?

   ____

   ____

   ____

   ____

4. Do you model authenticity?

   Most of the time   Sometimes   Seldom

   How well do people know you? Do you give them opportunities to see what God has done in your life? Most importantly, how open are you with your Father?

   ____

   ____

   ____

   ____

If a number of these areas need improvement, choose just one for now. Take a few moments to pray and then jot down one or two things you can do to make a difference.

____

____

____

____

____

____

____

Chapter 6

WHAT'S A NEW COVENANT MINISTRY?

2 Corinthians 3

S*uccess*.

We love the sound of that word, don't we? And we love the images it brings to mind, the thoughts of efforts fulfilled. Losing twenty pounds . . . shaving points off our golf game . . . opening our own business.

And we know success when we see it. Successful people are usually well educated, impeccably groomed, and financially prosperous. They exude the self-confidence that comes from a history of high achievement, and whatever they do, they do it well. And secretly—or not so secretly—we want to be like them. In fact, a good portion of our efforts is spent striving in their direction.

There's nothing wrong with setting goals and accomplishing dreams. There's nothing wrong with looking your best or achieving prosperity. But we need to understand that these things have nothing to do with success the way God measures it. The world may be impressed with such things, but God has a different standard.

A Popular Yet Incorrect Concept of Success

If anyone was ever dressed for success, it was Paul:

> Although I myself might have confidence even in the flesh. If anyone else has a mind to put confidence in the flesh, I far more: circumcised the eighth day, of the nation of Israel, of the tribe of Benjamin, a Hebrew of Hebrews; as to the Law, a Pharisee; as to zeal, a persecutor of the church; as to the righteousness which is in the Law, found blameless. (Phil. 3:4–6)

Paul was as well-heeled as they come. His ancestry was impressive (v. 5a); his orthodoxy, impeccable (v. 5b); his activity, incredible (v. 6a); his morality, immaculate (v. 6b). No doubt, his graduating class would have voted him "Most Likely to Succeed."

But once Paul came into contact with Christ, he saw his achievements in a different light:

> But whatever things were gain to me, those things I have counted as loss for the sake of Christ. More than that, I count all things to be loss in view of the surpassing value of knowing Christ Jesus my Lord, for whom I have suffered the loss of all things, and count them but rubbish so that I may gain Christ, and may be found in Him, not having a righteousness of my own derived from the Law, but that which is through faith in Christ, the righteousness which comes from God on the basis of faith. (vv. 7–9)

These are not the words of a modest man; these are the words of a transformed man—transformed by Jesus Christ, where the old things have passed away, and all things have become new (2 Cor. 5:17).

An Unpopular Yet Correct View of Success

It's easy to think that the better our qualifications, the more God can use us. In Philippians 3, Paul showed the inadequacy of human accomplishment. But in 2 Corinthians 3, he completed the picture. Here we discover where our adequacy for service really comes from. Before we go there, though, let's see how Paul set the message up.

In the last paragraph of 2 Corinthians 2, Paul said that he came in triumph, in the fragrance of Christ, and in sincerity. A skeptic could read those words and think Paul was bragging, drawing attention to himself. But in 3:1, Paul addressed that skepticism:

> Are we beginning to commend ourselves again? Or do we need, as some, letters of commendation to you or from you?

In those days, itinerant evangelists would often travel with letters of endorsement and recommendation, which functioned as a seal of approval upon their ministry. But Paul said his credentials were different:

> You are our letter, written in our hearts, known and read by all men; being manifested that you are a letter of Christ, cared for by us, written not with ink

but with the Spirit of the living God, not on tablets of stone but on tablets of human hearts. (vv. 2–3)

Paul didn't need a letter of approval. If anyone wanted to see whether his ministry was valid, they could look at the members of his scattered congregations. Their changed lives were all the commendation he needed. He acknowledged, though, that his successful ministry was not due to his work, but Christ's:

> Such confidence we have through Christ toward God. Not that we are adequate in ourselves to consider anything as coming from ourselves, but our adequacy is from God. (vv. 4–5)

So often we work overtime to get people to notice us, to show them how adequate we are, how competent, how gifted, how important. But it's not important that they see us, only Him. And our impressive qualifications and accomplishments only obscure the view.

A Series of Contrasts

Verses 5–11 delineate several contrasts that help us sort out our motives for serving God. They fall into two broad categories: the old arrangement of the flesh and the new arrangement of the Spirit.

> Not that we are adequate in ourselves to consider anything as coming from ourselves, but our adequacy is from God, who also made us adequate as servants of a new covenant, not of the letter but of the Spirit; for the letter kills, but the Spirit gives life.
>
> But if the ministry of death, in letters engraved on stones, came with glory, so that the sons of Israel could not look intently at the face of Moses because of the glory of his face, fading as it was, how will the ministry of the Spirit fail to be even more with glory? For if the ministry of condemnation has glory, much more does the ministry of righteousness abound in glory. For indeed what had glory, in this case has no glory because of the glory that surpasses it. For if that which fades away was with glory, much more that which remains is in glory. (vv. 5–11)

Our Access to Glory

Let's go back over the verses and note the contrasts:

verse	The Old/The Self	verse	The New/The Spirit
5	"adequate in ourselves"	5	"adequacy is from God"
5	"coming from ourselves"	6	"servants of a new covenant"
7	"letters engraved on stones"	2	"letter, written in our hearts"
7–9	"ministry of death . . . condemnation"	8–9	"ministry of the Spirit . . . righteousness"
11	"that which fades away"	11	"that which remains"

Under the Old Covenant, the Mosaic Law, God's truth was external—etched in tablets of stone. As such, it had only the power to condemn, not to give life.

After Jesus died, however, His life-giving Spirit was placed in our hearts. Since then, truth has been internal. The Law served to show us our inability to meet God's standard, but His Spirit in us makes us adequate to meet any requirement.

This means we are not to approach the Law to fulfill it but to come to Christ and let Him live His life through us. That's the glory of it all!

For sake of illustration, think of glory as light. There is a certain glory of the moon and stars that shine at night. But when the sun comes up in the morning, these stellar luminaries pale. Why? Because the glory of the sun outshines that of the moon and stars.

Similarly, the Old Covenant, with all its glory, paled with the dawn of Christ. This age ushered in a fresh and radiant confidence:

> Therefore, having such a hope, we use great boldness in our speech. (v. 12)

When Moses received the Ten Commandments on Mount Sinai, his face glowed from being in the presence of God. After he came down from the mountain, Moses veiled his face. He did this, at least initially, because the people were afraid (Exod. 34:29–35). But 2 Corinthians 3:13 indicates that he kept it on to cover up the fact that the glory was fading, to veil his own inadequacy:

> And [we] are not like Moses, who used to put a veil over his face so that the sons of Israel would not look intently at the end of what was fading away.

Regarding Moses, the veil represents an attempt to protect and preserve one's reputation—something we all do from time to time, though needlessly, now that our adequacy is in Christ. Regarding the Jews, the veil represents a blindness to the realities that the Old Covenant foreshadowed:

> But their minds were hardened; for until this very day at the reading of the old covenant the same veil remains unlifted, because it is removed in Christ. But to this day whenever Moses is read, a veil lies over their heart; but whenever a person turns to the Lord, the veil is taken away. (vv. 14–16)

The Secret of Confidence

When we come to Jesus, our lives are transformed. We come to the cross confessing our own inadequacy; we go away claiming only His adequacy. Like the hymnist said, "Nothing in my hand I bring, Simply to Thy cross I cling."[1]

If we strip away the veil, our glory is also ephemeral, fleeting, fading. Then what is the secret of our confidence? Look at verses 17–18:

> Now the Lord is the Spirit, and where the Spirit of the Lord is, there is liberty. But we all, with unveiled face, beholding as in a mirror the glory of the Lord, are being transformed into the same image from glory to glory, just as from the Lord, the Spirit.

The source of confidence is no longer ourselves but His Spirit. No longer do we need to live imprisoned in fear because we are free to live by His power. No longer do we need to be concerned about transforming ourselves; we can simply cooperate with being transformed by the power of His Spirit.

Two Essential Yet Overlooked Ingredients

The Holy Spirit is completely able to transform us into Christ's image, but two elements of this transformation are often overlooked.

True spirituality comes from God; it doesn't come from us. We can make ourselves available. We can take away the veil of false piety.

1. Augustus M. Toplady, "Rock of Ages, Cleft for Me," *Worship and Service Hymnal for Church, School, and Home* (Chicago, Ill.: Hope Publishing Co., 1957), no. 223.

We can choose to walk by the Spirit instead of by the flesh. But, in the final analysis, only He has the power to energize that walk. As Paul said in Galatians 2:20, "I have been crucified with Christ; and it is no longer I who live, but Christ lives in me." To be truly changed, we must rely on Him.

True spirituality takes time to develop; it doesn't happen overnight. From quick-stop convenience stores to cosmetic makeovers, we're used to instant results. It's easy to assume that God, especially a God of miracles, specializes in instant discipleship. But that is not the case. Heaven never hangs out the sign: Overnight Transformations. Inquire Within.

Like Paul, we can have a New Covenant ministry—a ministry guided by God's Spirit, carried out through our voice and hands and feet. But only if we get our ego, our pride, our need for attention out of the way . . . and let His glory shine through.

Living Insights

True spirituality comes from God, not us. And it takes time to develop—it doesn't happen overnight. Sometimes the changes come so gradually that the progress is hard to see. But with hindsight, we're often surprised and delighted to realize the differences we see in our spiritual maturity. Take a few moments to look back over your years of knowing Christ. What evidence can you see that He has been at work in the last . . .

Five years?

____

____

____

Ten years?

____

____

____

Twenty years?

____

____

____

If you can see signs that the Spirit has been at work, stop now and thank Him for what He's done. If you can't see much development, consider this. The Holy Spirit's power is limitless, but His freedom to work in our lives can be curtailed by the choices we make. To what degree are you abiding in Christ (John 15:1–8)? How deliberately and consistently do you study His Word and pray? Without your desire and participation, the Holy Spirit's hands are, so to speak, tied.

Will you make a commitment now to take your spiritual growth seriously? What will that commitment entail?

____

____

____

____

____

Chapter 7

CHECKLIST FOR AN EFFECTIVE MINISTRY

2 Corinthians 4:1–6

What if the apostle Paul had fallen asleep in the first century and then awoke, like Rip Van Winkle, in the twenty-first? Can't you see him stumbling around in amazement, rubbing his eyes in disbelief at the changes? And it wouldn't be just the technological changes that would astound him!

Paul saw the first baby pictures of the church; he cared for it in its infancy and dreamed what it could become. What would he think of its adult state? Does it look as he envisioned it?

As the premiere apostle of the early church, Paul wrote the first minister's handbook. How would today's ministries and pastors hold up under the guidelines he set forth?

We can't really answer that question without thoroughly examining the criteria. What *does* an effective ministry look like? Paul painted a picture of it for us in 2 Corinthians 4. Let's hold up the parent church to its offspring and see how well we compare.

Ministry Today: A Study in Confusion

If you have to admit, honestly, that you really don't know the criteria for an effective ministry, you're not alone. Few do. Why? Because the standards aren't often clearly taught. More often, "biblical standards" are merely masked personal opinions. *Moral purity*, for instance, takes on as many definitions as there are people—yet the Bible doesn't mince words on God's definition of it. Today's church faces a *rarity of biblical instruction*, and it breeds the spiritual confusion so many are experiencing.

Another reason for confusion is the *overemphasis on emotional persuasion* that pervades body life. The desire to change hearts often materializes in emotional manipulation, though often planned with the best intentions. Video presentations tug at heartstrings but sometimes oversimplify situations . . . three-ring circuses draw people to church but offer little substance for their souls . . . and preachers cultivate the pitch and rhythm of sermon presentations to keep congregations interested. Though these tactics often produce results, the commitment dies down with the excitement.

Perhaps these misguided efforts have contributed to the most devastating source of confusion: the *breakdown of personal integrity* in Christian leaders. It's much easier to look good than to be good, as many have discovered. But once you take away the lights, cameras, and microphone, too often you find dishonesty and hypocrisy lurking in the wings.

Because we want people to embrace Christianity, we're tempted to package it in an appealing box. But like supermarket cereal, the more energy we expend on bright packaging and gimmicks, the less likely it is that we'll offer genuine nourishment. Sugarcoated Christianity contains as many empty calories as a box of frosted breakfast flakes—and when the hype is over, it leaves people hungry.

Ministry as God Intended It

Ministers of God's Word ought to clear a path through the confusion. Let's turn to Paul's letter to learn God's standards for effective ministry.

A Correct Mentality

Second Corinthians 4:1 gives us a foundation:

> Therefore, since we have this ministry, as we received mercy, we do not lose heart.

What ministry was Paul talking about? He described it in chapter three—the ministry of the Spirit (vv. 4–11). It's the freedom available in Christ, the transformation into Christlikeness in the lives of believers. As Christ has offered these things to us, so we are to offer them to others. But a ministry needs certain qualities to do this effectively, and they arise naturally when we reflect on His gift of mercy.

First, *an effective ministry requires a right philosophy*. It must be a ministry with the openness, liberty, and authenticity 2 Corinthians 3 describes. A ministry without veils—without anything to hide and without anything to prove.

Second, *an effective ministry includes an abundance of mercy*. Mercy, someone once said, is God's ministry to the miserable. When we floundered without help, God came to our rescue. And because He helped us, we help others.

Third, *an effective ministry provides consistent stability*. A ministry as God intended isn't one that causes us to lose heart. Instead of dragging us down, it lifts us up. It doesn't depress us; it motivates us (see 4:16).

An Inspired Methodology

Though a correct mentality sets us on the right path, it must eventually translate into action. In verses 2–4, Paul delineated how our lives reflect effective ministry, and he offered himself as an example:

> We have renounced the things hidden because of shame, not walking in craftiness or adulterating the word of God, but by the manifestation of truth commending ourselves to every man's conscience in the sight of God. And even if our gospel is veiled, it is veiled to those who are perishing, in whose case the god of this world has blinded the minds of the unbelieving so that they might not see the light of the gospel of the glory of Christ, who is the image of God.

First, *Paul modeled rejection of deceit*. He used the phrase "things hidden" to indicate the secretive and underhanded nature of deception. With Paul, what you saw was what you got; he remained the same person in public and in private. And he urged us to do the same.

Second, *he was unwilling to rely on cleverness*. Our wit and charm don't aid the kingdom of God. The Lord doesn't use gimmicks in order to get results, nor does He play on people's emotions. He represents the plain, unvarnished truth of the gospel at all times.

Third, *Paul refused to mishandle Scripture*. In fact, *adulterating* is the word he used. An adulterer introduces a foreign element into something sacred and then continues about business as though the unfaithful act didn't take place. Applying this to the Scriptures, Paul taught that an effective minister remains faithful to the sacred intentions of God and avoids reading into the text or twisting it to prove a point.

Fourth, *he reached out to touch everyone's conscience*. That's all the Holy Spirit needs to perform surgery on our hearts—just the clean, sharp knife of the Word:

> For the word of God is living and active and sharper than any two-edged sword, and piercing as far as the

> division of soul and spirit, of both joints and marrow, and able to judge the thoughts and intentions of the heart. And there is no creature hidden from His sight, but all things are open and laid bare to the eyes of Him with whom we have to do. (Heb. 4:12–13)

We need to be a "manifestation of the truth" to others. Veering clear of manipulation and guilt-inducing tactics, it's our job to share the truth of the gospel, and it's God's job to change hearts.

Fifth, *Paul realized that some will not believe*. The "god of this world" has blinded men, and our efforts to share the Light may go unnoticed as a result. The great news, though, is that God has the ability to restore their sight.

An Authentic Model

In 2 Corinthians 4:5–6, Paul went on to describe his own approach to ministry:

> We do not preach ourselves but Christ Jesus as Lord, and ourselves as your bond-servants for Jesus' sake. For God, who said, "Light shall shine out of darkness," is the One who has shone in our hearts to give the Light of the knowledge of the glory of God in the face of Christ.

In these verses, we see four characteristics of an effective minister of God.

- Not proclaiming oneself as Lord
- Lifting up Christ as Lord
- Being a servant
- Giving God the glory and pointing others to Christ

Any leader, spiritual or otherwise, can easily become a hero in the eyes of those he leads—but the danger begins when he starts believing it himself! Paul continually pointed to Jesus Christ as Lord, never allowing those he taught to view him as anything more than a signpost. We see this attitude modeled in Acts 14, when he and Barnabas healed a lame man in Lystra. Those who saw the miracle thought the apostles were gods, and they wanted to offer up sacrifices to them (vv. 11–13).

> But when the apostles Barnabas and Paul heard of it, they tore their robes and rushed out into the crowd, crying out and saying, "Men, why are you doing these things? We are also men of the same nature as you, and preach the gospel to you that you should turn from these vain things to a living God, who made the heaven and the earth and the sea and all that is in them." (vv. 14–15)

Paul was appalled that the people of Lystra wanted to worship him. Far from requiring special treatment, he pitched in and worked alongside those to whom he ministered, going so far as to call himself their "bond-servant." He had one goal and one goal only: to point others to Christ.

How do you know when you've let pride creep into your ministry? When you talk about yourself often. When you expect special treatment. When you pursue promotion. When you expect others to follow you blindly and submissively. And when you resist accountability and vulnerability with others. When these attitudes crop up in your life, it's time to step down until the Lord regains firm authority. And when you see these attitudes in other leaders, run the other way.

Ministry Questions That Must Be Asked

How do today's ministers live up to Paul's example? Think about the leaders in your life. Do they exemplify the characteristics we've studied? In selecting someone to mentor you in the faith, have you chosen well?

What about you? Like it or not, you became a light for others to follow once you became a Christian. How brightly does your light shine?

No one is perfect. In fact, no one even comes close. The one quality that truly matters is our persistent, consistent desire to acknowledge Christ's authority—to make ourselves windows through which He is seen.

Living Insights

We can't help but examine ourselves as we read of Paul's fervent defense of Christ rather than himself. Look back over the characteristics Paul promoted for effective ministers in this chapter. Do you see any weaknesses in yourself that need strengthening? Which of the following characteristics need the most shoring up? Circle one or two that you can work on.

A *right philosophy*

An *abundance of mercy*

A *consistent stability*

A *rejection of deceit*

An *unwillingness to rely on cleverness*

A *refusal to mishandle Scripture*

An *appeal to everyone's conscience*

A *realization that some will not believe*

A *steadfast submission that points to Christ's lordship*

Paul wrote, "For God, who said, 'Light shall shine out of darkness,' is the One who has shone in our hearts . . ." (v. 6). In what ways can you let the Lord shine more through you in the area(s) you circled?

____

____

____

____

In the following space, jot down a prayer asking the Lord to shine His light brightest in the shadows of your life and strengthen you where you feel weak.

____

____

____

____

Chapter 8

POWER IN POTS . . . LIFE IN DEATH

2 Corinthians 4:7–12

Who doesn't like to make a good impression? To appear "together," in control? Christian or not, we all do. In fact, we expend a good bit of effort toward that end. Yet, paradoxically, the One who is truly the most impressive, the most in control, did virtually nothing to enhance His image at the moment all eyes were on Him.

Think of it. There He was, hanging on a cross, humiliated and in pain, all because He had called Himself God. And He *was* God! All the power in the world rested at His fingertips. Angels awaited the mere hint of His request. He could have ended his misery and proven His case in one fell swoop. But He didn't. Instead, He let the life drain out of His body. He let His friends bury Him in a borrowed grave, and He let His mockers trail away in self-congratulation.

Why? Even if not for His own comfort, wouldn't it have been better for His ministry to have shown everyone, once and for all, who He was and what He could do?

Is it any wonder the Cross is a stumbling block to so many people? As Paul wrote, "The word of the cross is foolishness to those who are perishing, but to us who are being saved it is the power of God" (1 Cor. 1:18).

The power of God. Once displayed in the submission of the Cross, His power is displayed now in the frailty of our flesh in whom Christ dwells. Power in weakness—that's the topic for this study.

Power That Comes from God

In 2 Corinthians 4, we come to a passage that seems to hit us from left field. Previously, Paul had been discussing his ministry, showing us the elements that made it successful . . . and then, all of a sudden, he said,

> We have this treasure in earthen vessels. (v. 7a)

What treasure was he talking about? The Gospel, in the form of Jesus Christ (see 4:1–6). The New International Version says this treasure is stored in "jars of clay." By this, Paul meant human beings, including himself. We are the bearers of "the light of the gospel of the glory of Christ, who is the image of God" (v. 4b).

God could have displayed His light through angels, blasting their trumpets in the heavens. But instead, He chose us. As someone once said, "He has limited the proclamation of His message to human throats." We're honored to fulfill this privilege, but we often fight the "clay pot" part of it. Even in our churches, we work hard to impress each other, especially visitors. We try to handle the Scriptures with ease and finesse, we polish our services to perfection, and we try to downplay our flaws and patch up the cracks in our finish.

There may be an element of pride in all this effort, but much of it is motivated by our earnest desire to minister as effectively as possible. Remember, though, this idea of "earthen vessels" fits Paul's description of a successful minister.

It's not that God is pleased with a shoot-from-the-hip approach to ministry. He delights in thoroughness, hard work, and even excellence (see Col. 3:23). So, why would He entrust the precious gospel to such mundane, fragile, flawed vessels?

The rest of 2 Corinthians 4:7 helps us understand:

> That the surpassing greatness of the power will be of God and not from ourselves. (v. 7b)

Like Mary's expensive perfume (John 12:3), the fragrant presence of Christ inside our hearts cannot be experienced by others until it is poured out. And often God pours out that fragrance by breaking the earthen vessel that holds it.

The next two verses tell not only how Paul felt but how we often feel:

> We are afflicted in every way, but not crushed; perplexed, but not despairing; persecuted, but not forsaken; struck down, but not destroyed. (2 Cor. 4:8–9)

The adjectives in this verse present poignant images. *Afflicted* carries with it the idea of pressure, as when grapes are squeezed dry by a winepress. *Perplexed* means "without a way" and suggests the feeling of being lost or disoriented. William Barclay puts this spin on the passage: "We are sore pressed at every point but not hemmed in . . . persecuted by men but never abandoned by God . . . at our wit's end but never at our hope's end . . . knocked down but not knocked out."[1]

Christ is never more visible in us than when others can find no other explanation for our hope and endurance through trials. Let's not forget that clay pots are made for use—use in representing Christ—and not to be kept on a shelf for display purposes only.

Life That Is in Jesus

Power in pots. That's one paradox of the Christian life. We come now to another paradox: Life in death. Experiencing the life of Jesus requires an acceptance of death.

> Always carrying about in the body the dying of Jesus, so that the life of Jesus also may be manifested in our body. For we who live are constantly being delivered over to death for Jesus' sake, so that the life of Jesus also may be manifested in our mortal flesh. (4:10–11)

What on earth did Paul mean when he said we carry about the death of Jesus in our living bodies? Or that while we live, we are constantly dying so that the life of Jesus (who is dead) can show up?

The first part isn't difficult to explain. In our hearts, we hold the results of Christ's death on the cross: salvation. And as He transforms us, or sanctifies us, we display Him and His salvation in our lives (Rom. 12:1–2).

To make sense of the second part of that verse, it helps to understand what Paul meant by the word *death*. He didn't mean a literal death, although that will eventually be part of it. He meant the cracking, or even shattering, of our pots. He meant being afflicted, perplexed, persecuted, struck down (see 2 Cor. 4:8–9). These things are part of the growth process in the Christian life (see James 1:2–4), and they are one of the chief means by which Christ is shown to the world.

When we die, He lives. When we lose, He wins. When we're weak, He's strong. When we're dependent, He's powerful. That's the beauty of clay pots—they allow the power of God's message to leak out. When our weakness shows, people realize it isn't the pot that's significant—it's God's power within that counts.

When other people see this "death" in us, it changes them.

1. William Barclay, *The Letters to the Corinthians*, rev. ed., The Daily Study Bible Series (Philadelphia, Pa.: The Westminster Press, 1975), pp. 198–200.

When the Corinthians saw it in Paul and his workers, it changed them, as Paul pointed out:

> So death works in us, but life in you. (2 Cor. 4:12)

Paradoxes That Must Be Remembered

A paradox is "a statement that is seemingly contradictory or opposed to common sense and yet is perhaps true."[2] First, when God displays His power, it flows through weakness. Second, when we model the death of Jesus, others see His life. And third, when the Cross is lifted high, even the arrogant are brought low. Because of these paradoxes, we know the outcome is sure even when it feels like we're losing. Our enemies will be defeated, even if they don't know it now.

Won't you answer the call of Christ as He beckons?

> "If anyone wishes to come after Me, he must deny himself, and take up his cross daily and follow Me. For whoever wishes to save his life will lose it, but whoever loses his life for My sake, he is the one who will save it." (Luke 9:23–24)

Living Insights

We've seen God's power displayed in the broken clay pots of our lives. Let's review some of the Bible characters who found this same principle to be true.

Think back over some of the Bible characters you've studied in the past. Many of them faced trials and even humiliation at times, and most of them came to see that God's power shone through their brokenness. Look up the following characters in your concordance or a Bible encyclopedia and fill in the chart as a reminder that great things can come from our worst moments.

Joseph

Trial: ____

____

2. *Merriam-Webster's Collegiate Dictionary*, 10th ed., see "paradox."

Results: ____

____

Ruth

Trial: ____

____

Results: ____

____

Job

Trial: ____

____

Results: ____

____

Daniel

Trial: ____

____

Results: ____

____

Now, think about your own life. What have been the hardest turns in your own road? Can you see increased maturity as a result of those times? What about your positive influence on others—has it increased or decreased as a result of those experiences?

____

____

____

____

____

The difficult times in your life, the cracks in your clay pot, are beautiful in the sight of God—that is, if you have allowed His fragrance to leak through them.

Do you want to make an impact where you work? Want to reach your school? Touch your neighborhood? Heal your family? Then live out the dying message of the Lord Jesus. Let it out. Don't hide your cracks, but let your humanity show. It's the cracks in the clay that allow people to see through and focus on the Lord. You'll be amazed at how often God honors a weak, broken piece of pottery.

Chapter 9

THE RIGHT FOCUS

2 Corinthians 4:13–18

There's a great story about an enthusiastic preacher and his congregation. One Sunday morning during a rousing sermon, the preacher shouted, "This church, like the crippled man, has got to get up and walk!"

The congregation, hanging on his every word, shouted back, "That's right, Reverend! Let it walk!"

The preacher continued, fervency mounting, "This church, like Elijah on Mount Carmel, has got to run!"

The congregation was right with him. "Let it run, preacher, let it run!"

The reverend went on, "This church has got to mount up with wings like eagles and fly!"

The congregation answered in chorus, "Let it fly, let it fly!"

The pastor leaned over his pulpit, sweat gleaming on his brow. "Now, if this church is gonna fly, it's gonna take money."

The congregation sat back. "Let it walk, preacher. Let it walk."[1]

When it comes to the Christian walk, most of us are pretty enthusiastic—until it gets uncomfortable. Until it costs too much financially, socially, or personally. How many of us could claim the epitaph Paul wrote for himself?

> I have fought the good fight, I have finished the course, I have kept the faith. (2 Tim. 4:7)

From his blinding start on the Damascus road to his binding shackles in a Roman dungeon, Paul was faithful to the end. Wouldn't you like to say that about yourself? That kind of resolve doesn't result from a New Year's resolution, a moment in time when anything seems possible and everything changes. It results from a moment-by-moment commitment to keep the right focus.

Realistic Motivation

Finishing the course isn't easy. The lanes are narrow; heartache,

1. See James S. Hewett, ed., *Illustrations Unlimited* (Wheaton, Ill.: Tyndale House Publishers, 1988), p. 459.

disappointment, and discouragement often jog alongside us. And there's a certain amount of self-sacrifice involved. But 2 Corinthians 4 is filled with nourishment that keeps us going—and holding the chapter together on both ends are two identical clauses that urge us forward. You can almost see the determined set of Paul's jaw as he wrote:

> We do not lose heart. (vv. 1, 16)

But why don't we lose heart? Is it sheer grit, pure willpower? Partly. But a good portion of Paul's motivation was the enormity of the task before him: "Since we have this ministry" (v. 1). What ministry? Establishing the church in the world—no small endeavor!

Realizing the weight of our task can spur us on. Winston Churchill realized this during World War II as he tried to give England a picture of the battle before her:

> Upon this battle depends the survival of Christian civilization. . . . The whole fury and might of the enemy must very soon be turned on us. Hitler knows that he will have to break us in this island or lose the war. . . . Let us therefore brace ourselves to our duties, and so bear ourselves that, if the British Empire and its Commonwealth last for a thousand years, men will still say: "This was their finest hour."[2]

In other words, "Don't lose heart, England! This battle is critical!" Whether we are the minister of a church or the mother of a teenager, perspective is the key to our stayed endurance.

Why, though, did the task matter to Paul? Because he owed a debt: "As we received mercy" (v. 1).

Jesus Christ, in His mercy, sacrificed His life to bring us salvation. In doing so, He also gave our lives purpose, direction, and meaning. Every worthwhile thing in our lives is a gift from Him. When we recognize this, what can we do but lay our lives down for Him in return? That debt was at the heart of Paul's motivation to keep running the race.

2. *Bartlett's Familiar Quotations*, 14th ed., rev. and enl., ed. Emily Morison Beck (Boston, Mass.: Little, Brown and Co., 1968), p. 921.

Enthusiastic Determination

We're motivated by the task before us and our debt of gratitude, but it takes determination to stay in the race. Sandwiched between the twin phrases of encouragement is a list of characteristics it takes to end well, not just begin well. We've discussed some of them: servanthood, humility, endurance, authenticity. Paul went on to name one more—enthusiastic determination:

> Having the same spirit of faith, according to what is written, "I believed, therefore I spoke," we also believe, therefore we also speak. (v. 13)

The phrase "what is written" indicates that the writer was quoting from another passage of Scripture, most likely the Old Testament. Here, Paul quoted from Psalm 116, a testament to his faith, given the trials he had recently experienced:

> It is particularly fitting that at this point Paul should quote from Psalm 116 precisely because it is a hymn of thanksgiving for deliverance from death: "The cords of death compassed me. . . . I found trouble and sorrow. Then called I upon the name of Jehovah. . . . I was brought low and He saved me. . . . Thou hast delivered my soul from death, mine eyes from tears, and my feet from falling. . . . I believed, and therefore I spoke. . . . Praise ye Jehovah."[3]

Like the psalmist, Paul had experienced God's faithfulness even in his time of suffering. And like the psalmist, he proclaimed it. It may have taken determination to continue on the path, but he did it. And he did it with enthusiasm.

But how can we hope to follow his example?

First, *enthusiastic determination grows out of being delivered by the Lord*. When we come to an impasse in life, with the Red Sea before us and a horde of Egyptians hot on our heels, nothing is more inspiring than seeing God part the waters before us. Unfortunately, like the Israelites, we tend to forget the Lord's deliverance when we're on safe ground again. Has the Lord seen you through a difficult

3. Philip Edgcumbe Hughes, *Paul's Second Epistle to the Corinthians* (Grand Rapids, Mich.: William B. Eerdmans Publishing Co., 1962), pp. 146–47.

time? Memorialize those events in your mind; revisit them often. They will give you hope when the waters grow rough again.

Second, *enthusiastic determination also grows when we focus on our future resurrection*. Paul continued his thought in 2 Corinthians 4:14:

> Knowing that He who raised the Lord Jesus will raise us also with Jesus and will present us with you.

There is no question that your heavenly Father will stay by your side no matter what you face. He may rescue you from physical danger, or He may permit you to die. But for the believer, death only transitions us into a better place. We have no reason to fear! Death closes the door on our earthly existence and opens the door of eternity. Claiming this with certainty removes terror and motivates us to keep going regardless of danger.

Not only is there a literal resurrection after we physically die, but there is also a resurrection in a figurative sense. When we die to ourselves and invest our lives in others, our faith is resurrected in them. Teachers are resurrected in their students; pastors, in their congregations; parents, in their children. That's what verse 15 promises:

> For all things are for your sakes, so that the grace which is spreading to more and more people may cause the giving of thanks to abound to the glory of God.

And this brings us to a third thought: *enthusiastic determination grows when we invest in the lives of others*. If you have lost heart, take a look at your life. Somewhere along the way, have you cloistered yourself away from others and drawn your focus inward? The life that reflects Christ's life lives to serve others (see Phil. 2:3–11).

Authentic Vision

In 2 Corinthians 4:16–18, Paul returned to where he started:

> Therefore we do not lose heart, but though our outer man is decaying, yet our inner man is being renewed day by day. For momentary, light affliction is producing for us an eternal weight of glory far beyond all comparison, while we look not at the things which are seen, but at the things which are not seen; for the things which are seen are temporal, but the things which are not seen are eternal.

You may not have noticed, but your "outer man" is decaying! Every day, your shoulders stoop a little lower, your hair grows a little grayer, your figure becomes a little less youthful. From the world's point of view, that's downright discouraging. You can't watch an evening of television without hearing a pitch for a product that can bring back your youthful luster. Why? Because without Christ, the outer man is all we have. But with the Holy Spirit in our lives, we have an "inner man" that is being renewed every day. That inner man never grows old and never dies—and knowing that puts our "momentary, light affliction" into perspective.

If we look only at the things that are seen, we'll be in the dumps before the day is done—guaranteed. The things that are unseen are eternal. Let's keep our focus off where we are and place it on where we're going. Look at life with a view on forever!

Specific Application

Finishing well . . . it's all in having the right focus. Keep in mind that today's deeds are threads woven into the tapestry of a bigger picture. Every kindness. Every thoughtful act. Every statement of witness. Every forgiving attitude. Every moment's investment. Every encouraging word. If you could see the eternal results, you'd never want to stop weaving!

Remember, too, that ordinary people are immortals in the making, and that we can contribute to their immortality. C. S. Lewis said:

> It is a serious thing to live in a society of possible gods and goddesses, to remember that the dullest and most uninteresting person you talk to may one day be a creature which, if you saw it now, you would be strongly tempted to worship, or else a horror and a corruption such as you now meet, if at all, only in a nightmare. All day long we are, in some degree, helping each other to one or other of these destinations. It is in the light of these overwhelming possibilities, it is with the awe and the circumspection proper to them, that we should conduct all our dealings with one another, all friendships, all loves, all play, all politics. There are no *ordinary* people. You have never talked to a mere mortal. Nations, cultures, arts, civilizations—these are mortal, and their life is to ours as the life of a gnat. But it is immortals whom

we joke with, work with, marry, snub, and exploit—
immortal horrors or everlasting splendours.[4]

So keep weaving. Keep investing. And keep dreaming of the unseen—no matter how dark and dreary the visible world appears. Then you'll have the kind of focus you need to keep running until the end.

Living Insights

If you could view the tapestry of your life right now, what do you think it would look like? Would the pattern be clear, the colors beautiful? Or would it be a confusing array of stitches and colors, zigzagging between God's plan and your own?

Take heart; the tapestry isn't finished. You can adjust your focus now and allow God to fashion the rest of the stitches according to His design, working your past blunders into its beauty. Review what we've learned from Paul in this lesson and see where your focus needs fine-tuning.

Realistic Motivation

How's your motivation level for finishing strong?

1	2	3	4	5	6	7	8	9	10
Discouraged				Ho-hum					Excited

If you need a little boost, try these two exercises:

1. Scan your local newspaper. What evidence do you find for godliness? What evidence do you find for Satan's influence?

____

____

____

2. Reflect on the twists and turns of your life. What do you remember of God's mercy during those times?

____

4. C. S. Lewis, *The Weight of Glory* (Grand Rapids, Mich.: William B. Eerdmans Publishing Co., 1965), pp. 14–15.

Enthusiastic Determination

How's your determination level?

1	2	3	4	5	6	7	8	9	10
Weak				So-so				Enthusiastic	

If your determination has been waning, ask yourself these questions:

1. Have your circumstances caused you to depend on the Lord, or have they tempted you to doubt Him?

2. Are you investing in others through teaching, prayer, or other ministries?

Authentic Vision

How's your vision for the future?

1	2	3	4	5	6	7	8	9	10
Dim				Blurry				Crystal clear	

If you're having difficulty facing the future with confident focus, reflect on these questions:

1. Does your thinking stop at the temporal, or do you weigh your experiences and actions in light of eternity?

2. What excites you about finishing the race and finishing well?

___

___

___

Satan would like nothing more than to distort your vision and call you out of the race. Don't let him sideline you. Get the finishing line in focus!

Chapter 10

HOPE BEYOND THE HEARSE

2 Corinthians 5:1–10

For all the technological advances of our time, two things in this life stand as firm as granite—birth and death. We can play around with the timing of those two events, but we are completely unable to eliminate the need for the one and the inevitability of the other. We're not much bothered by the birth issue, but death—that one we struggle with. Joseph Bayly comments:

> This frustrates us, especially in a time of scientific breakthrough and exploding knowledge, that we should be able to break out of earth's environment and yet be stopped cold by death's unyielding mystery. Electroencephalogram may replace mirror held before the mouth, autopsies may become more sophisticated, cosmetic embalming may take the place of pennies on the eyelids and canvas shrouds, but death continues to confront us with its blank wall. Everything changes; death is changeless.
>
> We may postpone it, we may tame its violence, but death is still there waiting for us.
>
> Death always waits. The door of the hearse is never closed.
>
> Dairy farmer and sales executive live in death's shadow, with Nobel prize winner and prostitute, mother, infant, teen, old man. The hearse stands waiting for the surgeon who transplants a heart as well as the hopeful recipient, for the funeral director as well as the corpse he manipulates.
>
> Death spares none.[1]

As Solomon told us in Ecclesiastes, death is the great equalizer (2:14; 7:2; 9:2–3). No matter who we are, no matter how much money we have, no matter how much influence we exert, death is inescapable. And because we cannot conquer death, we've come

1. Joseph Bayly, *The Last Thing We Talk About*, rev. ed. (Elgin, Ill.: David C. Cook Publishing Co., 1973), pp. 11–12.

up with all sorts of comfortable, though misconceived, theories to soften its impact.

Three Popular Misconceptions about Death

First, many people believe that death is a *temporary transition*—it simply moves us into a passing phase commonly called purgatory.[2] Ostensibly, purgatory is "an intermediate place between heaven and hell, where the unfinished business of earth is settled."[3] In this system of belief, others can pray someone out of this place of punishment, purification, and perfection.

Second, many seek release from death's permanent grip through *repeated reincarnation*. This Eastern philosophy holds that when we die, we can be born into another body. Recycling of the human spirit can go on indefinitely, bringing us to higher levels of happiness if we've lived a good life or lower levels of misery if we haven't.

And third, some believe that death is the *ultimate conclusion*, the grand finale to life. To them, an afterlife is nonexistent—this philosophy is what gave rise to the epicurean ethic: "Eat, drink, and be merry, for tomorrow we die."

The believers of these theories may be sincere, but they are sincerely wrong. The Scriptures clearly teach several truths about death: that it occurs to all (Eccles. 7:2); that it is the ultimate result of sin (compare Gen. 2:17 and 3:19 with Rom. 3:23); that we all will die once and that after death we will be judged by God (Heb. 9:27); and that when we die, if the chasm between us and God has not already been spanned by faith in Christ, it will then be unbridgeable (Luke 16:19–31, especially v. 26).

But that isn't all the Scriptures teach about death. If we're looking for reassurance about what happens when Christians die, Paul gave us the real answers in 2 Corinthians 5:1–10.

Scriptural Insights regarding Death

Paul's thoughts on death are definite:

> For we *know* that if the earthly tent which is our house is torn down, we have a building from God,

2. The word *purgatory* comes from the root word *purge*. It refers to a place of spiritual purging. Those who believe in purgatory support it with the apocryphal work of 2 Maccabees 12:39–45, along with Matthew 12:31–32 and 1 Corinthians 3:11–15.

3. David Steinmentz, "Purgatory," in *The New International Dictionary of the Christian Church*, rev. ed., ed. J. D. Douglas (Grand Rapids, Mich.: Zondervan Publishing House, 1978), p. 814.

> a house not made with hands, eternal in the heavens. (v. 1, emphasis added)

Isn't that comforting? When we face our own mortality or the loss of our loved ones, we can know with certainty, not wonder, what the future holds.

An Earthly Tent . . . an Eternal House

Paul used a familiar image to help his readers understand the unfamiliar: tents. He taught that in this life we have a "tent," an earthly body made of flesh and blood and bones. And when that tent is torn down—when we die—we will inhabit a new, everlasting dwelling.

Now, let's press this analogy a little bit. Have you ever spent time in a tent? If so, you know that it's a place where you'd only want to live for a short while. It's fun to camp out in a tent, but let's face it—you wouldn't want to call it home! It's hot in the summer, cold in the winter, and leaky when it rains. And the older it gets, the more it sags. Eventually, it frays and tears and rots. Paul expressed it pretty clearly:

> Indeed in this house we groan, longing to be clothed with our dwelling from heaven, inasmuch as we, having put it on, will not be found naked. For indeed while we are in this tent, we groan, being burdened, because we do not want to be unclothed but to be clothed, so that what is mortal will be swallowed up by life. Now He who prepared us for this very purpose is God, who gave to us the Spirit as a pledge. (vv. 2–5)

Physicians make their living listening to groaning tents. An orthopedic surgeon tries to keep the tent pegs from pulling loose, a dermatologist tries to keep the canvas in good shape, and general practitioners are always patching us up.

We groan because we are weary, rain-soaked campers longing for home (v. 2b). But when we shed this earthly tent from our shoulders, we will not be left naked and shivering (vv. 3–4). We will be clothed with immortality (1 Cor. 15:53–54). Like a huge down comforter, life—not death—will swallow us up (2 Cor. 5:4). To assure us of this, God gave us a deposit on our eternal home: the Holy Spirit (v. 5).

Absent from the Body . . . at Home with the Lord

Even greater than a new "tent" is the place it will be pitched, which was Paul's next word of encouragement to us:

> Therefore, being always of good courage, and knowing that while we are at home in the body we are absent from the Lord—for we walk by faith, not by sight—we are of good courage, I say, and prefer rather to be absent from the body and to be at home with the Lord.[4] (vv. 6–8)

While we are living in our earthly tents, we cannot have a tangible, visible, audible relationship with the Lord. We cannot walk by sight, so we walk by faith. But when we die, we will be at home with Him. We will hear His voice, touch His hands, see Him face-to-face. No wonder Paul preferred to be in heaven rather than here!

Our Present Ambition . . . Our Future Reward

Whether we live in these earthly, groaning tents or in an eternal building prepared for us by the Lord Himself, our goal should be the same:

> Therefore we also have as our ambition, whether at home or absent, to be pleasing to Him. (v. 9)

The anticipation of heaven naturally stirs in us an ambition to please the One who offers its glories to us. Hope motivates holiness. And as we aim to please God in this life, Paul assures us that God will reward us in the life to come.

> For we must all appear before the judgment seat of Christ, so that each one may be recompensed for his deeds in the body, according to what he has done, whether good or bad. (v. 10)

The Corinthian believers well understood the concept of a "judgment seat," or *bema*, in Greek. Paul himself had stood before the judgment seat of the Roman governor Gallio years before when hostile Jews accused the apostle of violating their religious laws (see Acts 18:12–17).

4. There is no mention of purgatory or any other kind of intermission here. If we are "absent from the body," we are "at home with the Lord."

The *bema* of Christ, however, is different. Christ will not judge believers to determine innocence or guilt, for we are all declared righteous in Him (see 2 Cor. 5:21). Our home in heaven is assured. At stake is our reward, which will be determined by the quality of our deeds (see also 1 Cor. 3:10–15) and the motives behind our deeds (see (1 Cor. 4:4–5).

Interestingly, Paul didn't say what will be the divine compensation —only that it will be in proportion to the deed itself, "whether good or bad." "The very things that we do, these we receive back," wrote commentator Paul Barnett.[5] Some false teachers in Corinth may have been teaching a popular Greek philosophy that only the soul mattered and sins of the body, such as sexual sins, were inconsequential. Paul's point here is that, although our tent is temporal, the "deeds of the body" are eternally important. Barnett summed up the thrust of Paul's message:

> The sure prospect of the judgment seat reminds the Corinthians—and all believers—that while they are righteous in Christ by faith alone, the faith that justifies is to be expressed by love and obedience (Gal. 5:6, Rom. 1:5) and by pleasing the Lord (2 Cor. 5:9). Our "confidence" that we will be "with the Lord" (v. 8) is to be held in tension with the "fear of the Lord" (v. 11), from which we serve Him.[6]

Essential Considerations before Death

Since many sincere people fall prey to popular misconceptions about death, let's focus on some divine truths that can equip us to help them be prepared for the inevitable.

First, *birth is an entryway to physical and spiritual life*. God designed it this way, for both the physical and spiritual realms. Jesus' discussion with Nicodemus made that clear: "Truly, truly, I say to you, unless one is born again he cannot see the kingdom of God" (John 3:3; see also 4–6). And we experience both physical and spiritual birth on *His* terms. Though we had no say in the beginning

5. Paul Barnett, *The Second Epistle to the Corinthians*, The New International Commentary on the New Testament Series, (Grand Rapids, Mich.: William B. Eerdmans Publishing Co., 1997), p. 275.

6. Barnett, *The Second Epistle to the Corinthians*, p. 277.

of our physical existence, our eternal life starts when we make the decision to be born again, through faith in Christ Jesus. So, *be certain you are born again*.

Second, *death terminates life*. Earthly life, that is. Life continues after our bodies die, it's just a question of where. Do you know where you'll be spending eternity? *Be sure you're ready to die*.

Third, *opportunity is limited to life*. Though life is short, it is eternally significant. There are no second chances once we die; there is no purgatory, no reincarnation. There isn't even nothingness. *Be certain you realize you have no options after you die*.

Death does not stop our existence. It only slips us from the realm of time into the timelessness of eternity. We will all live forever. It's not a question of existence; it's only a question of destination.

Do you know where you'll be?

Living Insights

Every human being has two divinely arranged appointments: birth and death. And if you are reading this today, you have already met one!

But there is another, perhaps more crucial appointment we all must meet. Hebrews 9:27 says, "It is appointed for men to die once and after this comes judgment." Death is a divine appointment.

The question is, are you ready? Have you received Jesus Christ as your Savior? If not, you can do that by calling on His name in prayer and receiving His gift of eternal life.

If you have lingering doubts or questions, you may wish to talk with a pastor or a Christian friend you trust. Do whatever it takes to settle this matter once and for all. Your eternal future depends on your decision.

If you are certain of your salvation, use this time to pray for others who are not.

Chapter 11

WHY CHRISTIANS ARE CONSIDERED CRAZY

2 Corinthians 5:11–21

Have you noticed that Christians are often considered a little crazy?

If your world is tightly knit with other Christians, you may have forgotten how other people view you. But all you have to do is turn on the morning news during a political segment to find out. We're not reasonable, according to secular standards. We're too conservative to be taken seriously. We're out there on the fringes. But, as A. W. Tozer pointed out, we have to admit that we do seem a little strange:

> A real Christian is an odd number anyway. He feels supreme love for One whom he has never seen, talks familiarly every day to Someone he cannot see, expects to go to heaven on the virtue of Another, empties himself in order to be full, admits he is wrong so he can be declared right, goes down in order to get up, is strongest when he is weakest, richest when he is poorest, and happiest when he feels worst. He dies so he can live, forsakes in order to have, gives away so he can keep, sees the invisible, hears the inaudible, and knows that which passeth knowledge.[1]

We may be a little strange, but at least we're in good company.

Who's in the Company of the Crazy?

Christians have been viewed as peculiar since the beginning (see 1 Pet. 2:9 KJV). Even Christianity's founder was considered crazy—in Mark 3, the multitudes said that Jesus had "lost his senses" (v. 21) and was "possessed" (v. 22), and in John 10, they said He had "a demon" and was "insane" (v. 20). So it's not surprising that his followers were regarded with the same contempt. For example,

1. A. W. Tozer, *The Root of the Righteous* (Camp Hill, Pa.: Christian Publications, 1986), p. 156.

after hearing Paul's testimony, King Agrippa told the apostle he was "out of his mind" (Acts 26:24). Hebrews 11 tells of the reaction others received:

> Others experienced mockings and scourgings, yes, also chains and imprisonment. They were stoned, they were sawn in two, they were tempted, they were put to death with the sword; they went about in sheepskins, in goatskins, being destitute, afflicted, ill-treated (men of whom the world was not worthy), wandering in deserts and mountains and caves and holes in the ground. (vv. 36–38)

Trace your way through history, and you'll find numerous individuals who were thought unbalanced because of their commitment to Christ. Think about those who laboriously copied out the Scriptures by hand before we had a printing press to do it. Imagine those who carried the torch of the Protestant Reformation, and all those who have given their lives as martyrs. Think of those who, even today, have given up lucrative careers to serve Christ in churches or on the mission field.

The world may think Christians are crazy, but reread the Hebrews passage to see how God describes His followers: "*men of whom the world was not worthy.*"

But if God is for us, why are so many in this world against us?

Why Are We So Misunderstood?

Someone has said that one of the most difficult things for Christians to endure is being misunderstood. Many find it so uncomfortable that they alter their behavior to avoid being viewed as "too Christian." Afraid of being seen as holier-than-thou or fanatical, afraid of losing acceptance at work or in the neighborhood or at school, they hide the Gospel inside and try to look just like they did before. And in those cases, Christians who are really living the Christian life look crazy even to other believers.

Why do we look so crazy to the rest of the world? There are four main reasons, and we can see what they are as we read the next passage of Paul's second letter to the Corinthians. Written in the context of the preceding verse about judgment day (2 Cor. 5:10), Paul explained how we are to live as believers by explaining his own behavior. And his explanation makes clear just why we tend to look outlandish to the rest of the world.

Our Mission Is Unique

Most people think everyone should live life the way they want to—married or divorced, homosexual or heterosexual, religious or not religious. As long as they're not hurting anybody, we're told we should accept people as they are and leave them alone—let them think whatever they want to about God.

But Paul had a different take on the believers' responsibility to others:

> Therefore, knowing the fear[2] of the Lord, we persuade men, but we are made manifest to God; and I hope that we are made manifest also in your consciences. We are not again commending ourselves to you but are giving you an occasion to be proud of us, so that you will have an answer for those who take pride in appearance and not in heart. For if we are beside ourselves, it is for God; if we are of sound mind, it is for you. (vv. 11–13)

Instead of tacitly *accepting* others' beliefs, Paul made it his goal to *persuade* them to understand Christ. Now, that didn't mean becoming obnoxious in the process. In fact, he went to great lengths to win a hearing with people from all walks of life. Look at what he wrote in his earlier letter about just how far he'd go in order to get people to listen to him:

> For though I am free from all men, I have made myself a slave to all, so that I may win more. To the Jews I became as a Jew, so that I might win Jews; to those who are under the Law, as under the Law though not being myself under the Law, so that I might win those who are under the Law; to those who are without law, as without law, though not being without the law of God but under the law of

2. The fear referred to here is not intended to indicate a cowering, frightened fear of being clubbed by an angry God. Instead, it indicates an awesome reverence. Proverbs 1:7 states that "the fear of the Lord is the beginning of knowledge," and Proverbs 9:10 says that fear is "the beginning of wisdom." That is the kind of fear Paul meant.

> Christ, so that I might win those who are without law. To the weak I became weak, that I might win the weak; I have become all things to all men, so that I may by all means save some. (1 Cor. 9:19–22)

In this world of live-and-let-live attitudes, it seems strange and sometimes offensive when we take a stand for righteousness. But that's a chance we have to take if the Gospel is going to be spread.

Our Approach Is Different

Few people have a driving passion in life. They do whatever is expedient or pleasurable, living for their momentary interests. But Christians have a different approach to life. They are driven by an internal and supernatural force—the love of Christ:

> For the love of Christ controls us, having concluded this, that one died for all, therefore all died; and He died for all, so that they who live might no longer live for themselves, but for Him who died and rose again on their behalf. (2 Cor. 5:14–15)

Christ's love for us, and ours for Him, now define our lives. In the grip of this love, our outlook on the world changes. Three themes determine our choices and our paths: first, that Jesus Christ died for all; second, that since all people are dead spiritually, they all need someone—Jesus—to give them life; and third, that once we have given Him our lives, we no longer desire to live for ourselves, but for Him.

That's a crazy message to a world full of people looking out for number one. If we tell them number one is Jesus, they're likely to roll their eyes and start whistling the theme to *The Twilight Zone*.

Ours is a different approach, no doubt about it. We are not only different in our motivation but in our value system as well.

> Therefore from now on we recognize no one according to the flesh; even though we have known Christ according to the flesh, yet now we know Him in this way no longer. (v.16)

The world judges people according to how they look and what they have. But as believers, we see others through Christ's eyes. Instead of evaluating them by their appearances, we see through to their hearts. We are drawn to them by their need for the Savior.

And, often, they're drawn to us because of what we have to offer . . . even if we look a little crazy.

Our Life Is Transformed

Believers in Christ have not just turned over a new leaf or managed to carry out a New Year's resolution. They are truly changed inside—transformed:

> Therefore if anyone is in Christ, he is a new creature; the old things passed away; behold, new things have come. (v. 17)

The word "creature" comes from the Greek word *ktisis*, the root of which means "the act of creation" or "that which is created."[3] When Christ invades a life, He performs an act of creation. He brings into being something new. Before, our spirit was dead; now it is alive. And once this new life is born, it transforms us from the inside out, changing our priorities, our relationships, our actions. Only God can do this work in us, but once He has done it, He gives us the responsibility of sharing Him with others:

> Now all these things are from God, who reconciled us to Himself through Christ and gave us the ministry of reconciliation, namely, that God was in Christ reconciling the world to Himself, not counting their trespasses against them, and He has committed to us the word of reconciliation. (vv. 18–19)

God has commissioned us to show others that Jesus' death on the cross appeased God's anger toward sin and replaced it with His acceptance of sinners. Humans keep a running tab of sin, but Christ paid the debt and wiped the slate clean:

> When you were dead in your transgressions and the uncircumcision of your flesh, He made you alive together with Him, having forgiven us all our transgressions, having canceled out the certificate of debt consisting of decrees against us, which was hostile to us; and He has taken it out of the way, having nailed it to the cross. (Col. 2:13–14)

3. Walter Bauer, *A Greek-English Lexicon of the New Testament and Other Early Christian Literature*, 2nd ed. Revised and augmented by F. Wilbur Gingrich and Frederick W. Danker, from Walter Bauer's 5th ed., 1958 (Chicago, Ill.: University of Chicago Press, 1979), p. 455.

In a world of debits and credits—a world that keeps score—this message sounds downright crazy. We would never think of allowing someone to walk away from the debt they owe, but that's just what Christ did for us. Such a message can do nothing but intrigue those who hear it.

Our Role Is Unusual

We serve an authority the world doesn't see. In many ways, we're like ambassadors to a foreign country, living among the citizens of the land but obeying a different ruler. We speak a different language; we have different customs, traditions, cultures, and lifestyles; and we feel a bit like strangers, even though we've made this place our home for a short while. And, like ambassadors, our purpose is to help bridge the gap between our home and theirs.

Ambassadors represent their homeland and its messages and policies to the people among whom they live. Their country is judged by their actions. Their deeds are watched and their words are studied with special attention.

The same is true of us.

Our true home is heaven; our true authority is the Lord. And we represent Him to those around us . . . even though they don't acknowledge Him as King.

Richard John Neuhaus expresses the tension we feel in this role at times:

> We are premature ambassadors, having arrived at court before the sovereignty of our king has been recognized. It is awkward, of course, and our authority is very much in question.[4]

Despite our discomfort, we can't afford to give up or go with the flow. God longs to be reconciled with the people He created. He longs to lavish His love on them. The primary message He wants His ambassadors to spread is this:

> He made Him who knew no sin to be sin on our behalf, so that we might become the righteousness of God in Him. (2 Cor. 5:21)

4. Richard John Neuhaus, *Freedom for Ministry*, rev. ed. (Grand Rapids, Mich.: William B. Eerdmans Publishing Co., 1992), p. 71.

This verse is the heart and soul of the Gospel. Jesus, the perfect Lamb of God, was made a sin offering on our behalf, just as Isaiah had prophesied:

> But the Lord was pleased to crush Him, putting Him to grief, if he would render Himself as a guilt offering. (Is. 53:10a)

In the Hebrew sacrificial system, the guilt of the people transferred to the "guilt offering," and when the lamb was slaughtered, their sins were atoned. In a similar way, Jesus assumed our sin on the cross, bearing our condemnation so we could assume His righteousness. Through faith we become the righteousness of God. A legal transfer occurs at the Cross; we trade our guilt for His innocence. We are free!

How Can Crazy People Like Us Be Effective?

We may seem crazy to the world around us, but we're the only ones who know where we're going! In a world that has lost its way, we can shed some light on the path by doing three things.

First, *we need to maintain our mission*. Regardless of the raised eyebrows, we need to keep persuading others of the truth.

Second, *we need to maintain our perspective*. It's easy to be fooled by a flawless exterior, but no matter how successful and "together" some may appear on the surface, everybody needs the Lord. When we see through the Lord's lenses, we look past the face to the heart.

Third, *we need to fulfill our role as ambassadors*. R. V. G. Tasker gave us a succinct description of the job:

> "An ambassador . . . is at once a messenger and a representative. He does not speak in his own name. He does not act on his own authority. What he communicates is not his own opinions or demands, but simply what he has been commanded to say." . . . Ambassadors engaged upon human affairs are chosen especially for their tact, their dignity and their courtesy, and because they are gifted with persuasive powers. The ambassadors for Christ should show the same characteristics. They must never try to bludgeon men and women into the kingdom of

God, but must speak the truth in love . . . by the gentleness and meekness of Christ.[5]

Yes, we do seem weird to the world sometimes. But only until they realize that what appears to be weird is really wise and best . . . and exactly what they need.

Living Insights

We concluded this chapter with three things we need to focus on in order to have an impact in this world. Look at each in light of your own life, and measure your personal impact.

How would you define your main mission in life, truthfully? It may help to ask yourself what your thoughts tend to center on, where you spend your time, what kinds of relationships you have, and how you spend your money.

____

____

____

____

____

Think about the people with whom you regularly spend time or see during the week. What would you say their relationship with God is like? What influences your answer? Can you think of anyone whose outer appearance is different from the state of their heart?

____

____

____

____

____

5. R. V. G. Tasker, *The Second Epistle of Paul to the Corinthians* (Grand Rapids, Mich.: William B. Eerdmans Publishing Co., 1958), pp. 89–90

Whether you intend to be or not, you are an ambassador for Christ (v. 20). How well would you say you are representing Him to those around you? What things are you doing well? What things might you need to work on?

____

____

____

____

____

Do you ever feel like the people around you think you're crazy? If so, why? If not, why not? Your answer may reveal to you the extent of your impact. May your impact go as deep and spread as wide as the measure of Christ's love!

____

____

____

____

____

Chapter 12

A Realistic Portrait of Ministry

2 Corinthians 6:1–10

Do you ever wonder just what your minister does all week?

Some people envision their minister ensconced in his office, praying and studying, organ music playing softly in the background, with an occasional interruption by angelic visitations. And some days really are a little like that, at least for an hour or two! And when he's around us, we often think we need to reinvent our own lives—sound a little more pious, put the Bible out on the coffee table, hide any evidence of our ordinary lives.

Conceptions of ministry abound.

Familiar Concepts of Ministry

The most familiar concepts of ministry can be almost clerically sorted into three files. First, many think ministry is an ivory-tower existence. They think of it as a place of stained-glass solitude and knee-worn prayer. They envision long hours of poring over the Scriptures by candlelight and meditating in a musty study. They see it as a monastic place where angels traffic and organ music pipes in the background.

Second, many think of ministry as public manipulation and exploitation. These cynics look at the minister not as a pious monk but as a powerful mogul. He is pictured as one who likes to be in charge and unquestioningly followed.

Third, many think ministry is for an esoteric elite who have arrived spiritually and are models of perfection. This studio portrait of the ministry is too glowing and too flattering to be true. People in the ministry aren't perfect. They have wrinkles in their personality, age spots on some of their opinions, and a good share of sagging skin in their convictions. They aren't always loving or patient or unselfish or forgiving. Though ministers, they still are, in a word, human.

Necessary Commands to Ministers

Second Corinthians 5 states that if we have been reconciled to God, then we have been given a ministry of reconciliation (v. 18). It is a ministry God has committed to each of us, not to a select few (v. 19). All of us are His ambassadors (v. 20).

Therefore, the portrait people see of ministry is a portrait of *us*. To make that representation as positive as possible, Paul gave two commands to every minister, every Christian.

Command #1

Do not receive the grace of God in vain:

> And working together with Him, we also urge you not to receive the grace of God in vain—for He says,
> "At the acceptable time I listened to you,
> And on the day of salvation I helped you."
> Behold, now is "the acceptable time," behold, now is "the day of salvation." (6:1–2)

For several paragraphs Paul's letter urges us to model a New Covenant ministry, one that emphasizes the work of the Spirit as opposed to the work of the flesh. The work of the flesh is law-oriented; the work of the Spirit, on the other hand, is grace-oriented. The work of the flesh depends on self; the work of the Spirit depends on the Lord. The work of the flesh focuses on the external and the temporal; the work of the Spirit focuses on the internal and the eternal.

The "day of salvation" should never be relegated to a past-tense experience. It should be lived out *now*, in the present, as we live by grace instead of by law.

Are your life and your ministry grace-oriented or law-oriented? Are you living freely by grace, or are you so afraid of license that you've become a legalist? If the latter is true, then God's grace is in vain. Ministry should be lived out freely and authentically, not rigidly and touched up.

Command #2

Cultivate credibility in ministry:

> Giving no cause for offense in anything, so that the ministry will not be discredited, but in everything commending ourselves as servants of God. (vv. 3–4a)

How can we keep the ministry from being discredited? By not giving any cause for offense (v. 3a) and by being servants (v. 4a).

The Greek term for *discredited* is used only here and in 8:20. It means "to find fault or blame." The Hebrew equivalent is used in Proverbs 9:7 and is translated "dishonor."

The ministry can become discredited or dishonored when we break a promise, exploit people, live hypocritically, are unfaithful, compromise truth, become greedy, or expect special treatment.

Living out this ancient prayer will go a long way toward keeping our ministries from being discredited: "From the cowardice that shrinks from new truth, from the laziness that is content with half-truths, from the arrogance that thinks it knows all the truth, O God of truth, deliver us. Deliver me."

The apostle urged integrity in ministry. But practically speaking, how does all this get worked out on a daily basis?

Realistic Characteristics of Ministering

In 2 Corinthians 6:4b–10, we have one of the clearest, most realistic descriptions of how to minister with integrity.

Realistic Circumstances

Paul's words topple any ivory-tower image we might have constructed concerning ministry. He wrote that he ministered

> in much endurance, in afflictions, in hardships, in distresses, in beatings, in imprisonments, in tumults, in labors, in sleeplessness, in hunger . . . (vv. 4b–5)

That's not exactly the description you'd expect to read on a divinity school brochure! Granted, not all ministry encounters are like this. But ministers must prepare themselves for pleasant and unpleasant times. In a word, they must *endure*. The Greek word for *endurance* is *hupomonē*. William Barclay explains its meaning:

> It does not describe the frame of mind which can sit down with folded hands and bowed head and let a torrent of troubles sweep over it in passive resignation. It describes the ability to bear things in such a triumphant way that it transfigures them.[1]

1. William Barclay, *The Letters to the Corinthians*, rev. ed., The Daily Study Bible Series (Philadelphia, Pa.: The Westminster Press, 1975), pp. 212–13.

If anyone has ever endured hardships for the sake of ministry, it's Paul. But because he set up his life as a model to others, we can learn from the various trials he endured.

First, he battled inner struggles—afflictions, hardships, and distresses. His *afflictions*, or "pressures" as the Greek root renders it, included concerns that pressed in and weighed him down. His *hardships* required that he do without those things that make life comfortable and secure. And his *distresses*, or "narrow places," pushed him into tight spots, where he felt cornered and trapped.

Paul also experienced external troubles—beatings, imprisonments, and tumults. His *beatings* were "physically torturous," his *imprisonments* were numerous, and his exposures to *tumultuous situations* landed him in the midst of violence, public outcries, and assaults.

And, finally, Paul endured the private disciplines of commitment to the cause—labor, sleeplessness, and hunger. He worked tirelessly and without ceasing to spread the gospel through the land, but he counted it all expedient for the joy of the Cross (see 11:23–28; compare 4:7–12; 12:15).

How did Paul remain committed to the ministry and encouraged at heart while facing such torrential circumstances? And how can we adopt his attitude when we face similar ones? The next few verses provide an umbrella of attitudes to safeguard us against life's inclement situations.

Realistic Qualities

In 6:6–7, Paul listed nine qualities that protected him in the stormy times:

> In purity, in knowledge, in patience, in kindness, in the Holy Spirit, in genuine love, in the word of truth, in the power of God; by the weapons of righteousness for the right hand and the left.

Four of these attributes are external attitudes, visible to other people: (1) purity, a clean lifestyle; (2) knowledge, a practical awareness of truth; (3) patience, a calm in the midst of storms; and (4) kindness, a softness opposed to severity and meanness.

The remaining five wield their power in the hidden places of the heart: (1) the Holy Spirit, our deepest source of strength; (2) a genuine love for others that prompts our sacrificial giving; (3) the Word of Truth we treasure in our hearts and offer to others; (4) the power of God for endurance and provision; and (5) the weapons of righteousness, detailed in Ephesians 6:10–17.

Surely, if we exude these qualities in our personal lives and our ministries, the results will be nothing short of tremendous, right?

Realistic Results

Realistically, the results of our efforts will be mixed:

> By glory and dishonor, by evil report and good report. (2 Cor. 6:8a)

Paul's efforts were met with some successes, some lukewarm receptions, and some downright violent resistance to his outreach. In our own ministries, we can expect that some will respect and respond to us while others will resent us. Some will adore us; some will wish they never knew us. But we're in good company. Not only Paul but also Jesus experienced the same thing (see Mark 14:1–6).

Realistic Images

Sometimes it's hard to know what image we project to others as Christians—especially if we've chosen ministry as our vocation. Truly, we don't need to be anything other than who and what we are. But what we are is a study in contrasts. We are

> regarded as deceivers and yet true; as unknown yet well-known, as dying yet behold, we live; as punished yet not put to death, as sorrowful yet always rejoicing, as poor yet making many rich, as having nothing yet possessing all things. (2 Cor. 6:8b–10)

The Living Bible words this verse in a way that hits closer to home:

> We stand true to the Lord whether others honor us or despise us, whether they criticize us or commend us. We are honest, but they call us liars. The world ignores us, but we are known to God; we live close to death, but here we are, still very much alive. We have been injured but kept from death. Our hearts ache, but at the same time we have the joy of the Lord. We are poor, but we give rich spiritual gifts to others. We own nothing, and yet we enjoy everything. Here's the bottom line: we don't need to worry

about our image. We live to show others the image of Christ, to be His ambassadors. What they think of us really doesn't matter, unless it gets in the way of their view of Him.

A Final Word on Ministry

A large group of people over the age of ninety-five were asked the question, "If you could live your life over again, what would you do differently?"

Their answers fell into three dominant categories. They said they would reflect more, risk more, and do more things that would live on after their death. As we put the final brushstrokes on this realistic portrait of ministry, take a look at the canvas of your own life. What do you see? What would you paint over if you had the chance?

What is your life amounting to? Are you playing everything safe? Will anything you're doing now live on after you die?

Ministering to others is a great way to invest your life. It's a life of reflection. It's a life of risks. And it's a way of leaving something behind.

Ministry is the noblest of endeavors. God had only one Son . . . and God chose for Him a life of ministry.

Living Insights

Unless you are in full-time Christian work, you probably don't think of your life in terms of ministry. But it is. Each moment of each day, you are impacting the work of Christ . . . either through pointing toward the gospel or obscuring it.

Review the circumstances of this past week. In what ways has Christ been evident in you? It might help to review Paul's list concerning effective ministers and see whether it characterizes your life lately. As you look over the following contrasts, make an X on the scale as it describes your life/ministry.

Impurity ____ Purity

Opinions ____ Knowledge

Pushiness	Patience
Taking advantage of others	Kindness
Absence of the Holy Spirit	Presence of the Holy Spirit
Selfishness	Genuine love
Deceptions	Truth
The power of the flesh	The power of God
Manipulation	Weapons of righteousness

Sadly, some Christians operate their ministries and live their lives closer to the left-hand side than the right. What can move a person toward the godly side? True repentance.

If you sense the need to confess your sin in a particular area, pause now and pray David's prayer of surrender in Psalm 139:23–24. Then turn to Psalm 130 and pray this confession. Experience the cleansing of God's forgiveness, then set out to make some changes in your life and ministry. Today is the day to start anew.

Chapter 13

Good Relationships and Bad Partnerships

2 Corinthians 6:11–18

The people who find life most satisfying have learned the secret of getting along with other people.

In fact, success in the workplace has more to do with social skills than with job skills. A study done at the Carnegie Institute of Technology showed that in the field of engineering, for example, about 15 percent of a person's financial success is due to technical knowledge. The rest, a full 85 percent, is due to the engineer's ability to relate well with people.[1] And Dr. William Menninger found that only 20 to 40 percent of people lose their jobs because they lack technical skills; the other 60 to 80 percent are discharged because they lack relational skills.[2]

Most of us spend our lives pursuing prestige and possessions, only to find that they leave us empty. Our relationships, or lack of them, truly determine our level of happiness. As Solomon put it,

> Better is a dish of vegetables where love is
> Than a fattened ox served with hatred. (Prov. 15:17)

Years ago, in a widely read book called *The Friendship Factor,* author and psychologist Alan Loy McGinnis told two stories that illustrate Solomon's point.

> One evening a neurosurgeon and I stood silently at the window, watching the lights of the city come on far below us. It was not easy for him to begin counseling. . . .
>
> Finally, he took a deep breath, like a man about to dive into a cold swimming pool, and said:
>
> "I guess I'm here because I'm messing up all my relationships. All these years I've fought to get to

1. Alan Loy McGinnis, *The Friendship Factor* (Minneapolis, Minn.: Augsburg Publishing House, 1979), p. 15.

2. McGinnis, *The Friendship Factor,* p. 15.

> the top of my profession, thinking that when I got there people would respect me and want to be around me. But it just hasn't happened."
>
> He crushed the empty Styrofoam cup in his fist, as if to emphasize his desperation.
>
> "Oh, I suppose I do command some respect down at the hospital," he went on, "but I'm not close to anybody, really. I have no one to lean on. But I'm not sure you can help me either—I've been shy and reserved all my life. What I need is to have my personality overhauled!"[3]

The next story, though, proves that personality wasn't the problem.

> Hubert never ran in influential circles. He grew shrubs and trees, working with his hands the plot of land left him by his father. He was anything but an extrovert.
>
> Yet when Hubert died, his funeral was the largest in the history of our little town. There were so many people that they filled even the balcony of the church.
>
> Why did such a shy man win the hearts of so many people? Simply because, for all his shyness, Hubert knew how to make friends. He had mastered the principles of caring, and for more than 60 years he had put people first. Perhaps because they recognized that his generosity of spirit was an extra effort for someone so retiring, people loved him back. By the hundreds.[4]

Down deep, we all want what Hubert had, don't we? People are important; we need them in our lives. Maybe we shouldn't be surprised that the Bible is so full of references to relationships. Virtually every page is swarming with people—people fighting, people planning, people praying, people laughing and singing, people grieving and sorrowing. And most of the time, they are doing it together.

3. McGinnis, *The Friendship Factor*, pp. 12–13. Reprinted by permission.

4. McGinnis, *The Friendship Factor*, p. 14. Reprinted by permission.

In the New Testament, we get to know one of the major characters of the Bible primarily through his relationships. By reading Paul's letters to the people in his life, we discover his personality. And in this study's passage, we see him addressing the issue of his relationship with the Corinthians. But before we move forward, let's take a look at what we've discovered so far in our study.

Where Have We Been?

Part of Paul's motivation in writing this letter was to clear up some problems in his relationship with the Corinthian believers. In his opening, he reiterated his commitment to them, then went on to clear up some misunderstandings in their view of him—remember, some people were upset that he had not visited them as he had hoped to do, and others thought that he was power-hungry.

Between 2 Corinthians 2:14 and 6:10, Paul digressed, writing at length about ministry and what makes it effective. But then he returned to his original train of thought and the purpose of his letter—the restoration of a relationship.

When Is It Right to Be Free?

In 6:11, Paul reminded the Corinthians about how freely he had given himself to them and how candid and honest he had been:

> Our mouth has spoken freely to you, O Corinthians, our heart is opened wide.

Literally, the end of this verse says, "our heart is enlarged." Chrysostom said, "Heat makes all things expand and the warmth of love will always expand a man's heart."[5] Paul's love for these people was real and deep; he'd made himself vulnerable in the way he cared for them. But they did not respond in kind:

> You are not restrained by us, but you are restrained in your own affections. (v. 12)

The term *affections*, from the Greek word *splagchna*, means "bowels." It literally refers to the upper viscera—that is, the heart, liver, and lungs. In ancient days, it was believed that the emotions

5. William Barclay, *The Letters to the Corinthians*, rev. ed., The Daily Study Bible Series (Philadelphia, Pa.: Westminster Press, 1975), p. 218.

emanated from these organs.[6] Paul was implying that the past emotions in their relationship had been one-sided, and now he was urging them to open their hearts to him in return:

> Now in a like exchange—I speak as to children—open wide to us also. (v. 13)

Have you ever tried to hug someone who didn't hug back? Tried to converse with someone who grunts in response? A relationship has to be a two-way street. Both parties have to freely share their feelings and open up in conversation for the relationship to work.

But on the heels of this admonition to be free and vulnerable, Paul talked about holding back.

When Is It Wrong to Be Bound?

There are times when it is appropriate to hold back in a relationship, when bonding with another person is actually discouraged. Paul said it in pretty straightforward terms:

> Do not be bound together with unbelievers. (v. 14a)

Many Christians today take this verse to mean more than Paul intended, choosing to associate only with other believers, and even using only Christian tradespeople for the services they need. But a glance at 1 Corinthians 5:9–10 assures us that this is not a prohibition against casual friendships with unbelievers:

> I wrote you in my letter not to associate with immoral people; I did not at all mean with the immoral people of this world, or with the covetous and swindlers, or with idolaters, for then you would have to go out of the world.

In fact, if we did not associate with the lost at all, how would they ever come to know Christ? The term "bound together" that Paul used in 2 Corinthians 6:14 is a reference to a yoke, like the one placed on oxen working as a team. In Deuteronomy 22:10, a similar term is used that helps us to understand Paul's meaning:

> "You shall not plow with an ox and a donkey together."

6. Barclay, *The Letters to the Corinthians*, p. 218.

Paul used the term figuratively, but the Deuteronomy passage uses it literally. Oxen and donkeys pull differently; hitching them together will cause problems. In the same way, it's a mistake to hitch together a believer and an unbeliever in a relationship that requires pulling together, whether it be a marriage relationship, a business partnership, or any other long-term cooperative effort. Believers and unbelievers have different goals, different outlooks. They're always going to be pulling against each other as a result of those differences.

But what if you are already married to an unbeliever? Maybe you, too, were a non-Christian when you married, or maybe you have only recently begun to take your faith seriously. Does that mean you are to become unhitched—divorced?

No. First Corinthians 7:13 overrides this command. It says that if your unsaved partner is willing to stay with you, you are to stay in the relationship and become a live-in witness for Christ. But it will not be easy. In fact, the struggles will sometimes be intense.

This whole discussion gives rise to an important question: What exactly constitutes being "bound"? How close is too close when it comes to unbelievers? Second Corinthians 6:14b–16a gives us the answer:

> For what partnership have righteousness and lawlessness, or what fellowship has light with darkness? Or what harmony has Christ with Belial, or what has a believer in common with an unbeliever? Or what agreement has the temple of God with idols?

Underscore the words *partnership*, *fellowship*, *harmony*, *common*, and *agreement*. If these words describe any of your relationships with non-Christians, you are likely on shaky ground. A saved person is fundamentally different from a lost person. You can have fondness and compassion for an unbeliever, and, hopefully, you have civility and kindness toward them. But if the relationship goes deeper than that, you are asking for trouble. It will eventually lead to a compromising of your convictions.

The underlying reason for this prohibition is found in verses 16b–18:

> For we are the temple of the living God; just as God said,
>
> "I will dwell in them and walk among them;

And I will be their God, and they shall be My
people.
Therefore, come out from their midst and be
separate," says the Lord.
"And do not touch what is unclean;
And I will welcome you.
And I will be a father to you,
And you shall be sons and daughters to Me,"
Says the Lord Almighty.

Our relationship with God involves spiritual harmony (v. 16b), personal purity (v. 17), and familial intimacy (v. 18). We are God's temple, and we should not bring into His temple anything or any relationship that does not honor that harmony, purity, or intimacy.

So, how can we make sure to stay on the straight and narrow path when it comes to relationships?

Safe Guidelines for Relationships

Two simple rules of thumb will help you stay on safe ground as you decide how close to get to the people in your life.

First, *unless there is an emotional bond, we cannot be free in a relationship*. No matter how much you would like to share a close relationship with another person, it cannot happen if the feeling isn't mutual—even if the other person is a believer. So guard your heart. Don't allow yourself to become more vulnerable than the other person is willing to become.

Second, *unless there is spiritual freedom, we dare not be bound in a partnership*. Unless your spiritual values and goals are in strong agreement, getting involved in a partnership of any kind—friendship, business relationship, or marriage—will be like yoking a donkey and an ox. You'll always be out of step with each other, and sooner or later, that yoke is going to chafe.

God has designed us for close relationships, but He means for them to be supportive, not painful. These guidelines help keep them pain-free at the fundamental level.

Living Insights

With whom do you have your closest relationships? Jot down the names here. Beside each, indicate whether you are equally or unequally yoked with this person.

1. ________________________________ O Equally Yoked
O Unequally Yoked

2. ________________________________ O Equally Yoked
O Unequally Yoked

3. ________________________________ O Equally Yoked
O Unequally Yoked

4. ________________________________ O Equally Yoked
O Unequally Yoked

5. ________________________________ O Equally Yoked
O Unequally Yoked

If you find yourself in close relationships with unbelievers . . .

What do you think has drawn you toward them?

____

____

____

Have you seen yourself compromise your spiritual values as a result of these relationships? If so, how?

____

____

____

If you lack close relationships with other believers, why do you think this is so?

____

____

____

What can you do to increase the number of "equally yoked" relationships in your life?

____

____

____

If your closest relationships are with other believers . . .

Thank the Lord for these blessings!

But also ask yourself whether, like Paul, any current misunderstandings need ironing out. If so, what actions can you take to make things right?

____

____

____

Also, ask yourself how much contact you have with the non-Christian world. Do you engage in casual relationships with unbelievers as salt and light in their lives (see Matt. 5:13)?

____

____

____

All our relationships ultimately exist for God's glory—either to shine as lights in a darkened world or to encourage and build up those within His body. Let's open ourselves up to be used by Him with whomever and whatever He places before us.

Chapter 14

REVERENCE FOR GOD, RESPECT FOR OTHERS

2 Corinthians 6:11–7:4

One of television's best-known interviewers, Barbara Walters, wrote a book years ago called *How to Talk with Practically Anybody about Practically Anything.* In it, she described the characteristic that virtually everyone finds most appealing:

> The most consistently endearing human trait is warmth. *Everybody* responds to the person who radiates friendliness from a serene core. Such people are lovely to be around because they don't reject or belittle and, best of all, they bring out the best, most generous qualities in the people they encounter.[1]

The world often feels like a pretty cold place. We crave the warmth of relationships like we crave the warmth of a fire after a day in the snow. And if we don't have it, we'll go to any lengths to obtain it.

The need for relationship, for closeness and acceptance, is what makes young people seek intimacy outside of marriage. It's what makes teenagers adopt dress styles and behaviors that identify them with a group—any group. It's what makes school children act out. They long for someone to notice them, to drop what they're doing and pay attention, to care. They want a relationship more than anything on earth . . . and so do you. All of us do. It's what we were designed for.

But just as a runaway can easily wander down the wrong alley in his search for a warm place to sleep, so all of us can be led astray if we take a wrong turn in the relationships we choose.

Guidelines for Fulfilling Relationships

In the last chapter, Paul gave us some guidelines for choosing our relationships. Let's review them before we continue. The first

1. Barbara Walters, *How to Talk with Practically Anybody about Practically Anything* (New York, N.Y.: Dell Publishing Co., 1970), p. 142.

one comes from 2 Corinthians 6:11–13:

> Our mouth has spoken freely to you, O Corinthians, our heart is open wide. You are not restrained by us, but you are restrained in your own affections. Now in a like exchange—I speak as to children—open wide to us also.

Guideline #1

Unless there is an emotional bond, we cannot be free in a relationship. The warmth in a relationship has to be felt on both sides for the relationship to function as it's meant to.

Paul's second piece of advice comes in verses 14–16a.

> Do not be bound together with unbelievers; for what partnership have righteousness and lawlessness, or what fellowship has light with darkness? Or what harmony has Christ with Belial, or what has a believer in common with an unbeliever? Or what agreement has the temple of God with idols? For we are the temple of the living God.

Guideline #2

Unless there is spiritual freedom, we dare not be bound in a partnership.

That can sometimes be a hard one. We know that it's important to share values and priorities in close relationships, whether they be friendships or marriage or business partnerships. But when loneliness overwhelms us or we're strongly attracted to other qualities a person possesses, it's easy to compromise. It becomes hard to remember why we should avoid being "unequally yoked" (v. 14 KJV).

But Paul reminded us of the answer. It's because "we are the temple of the living God" (v. 16). Our bodies are His house; His name is on our mailbox. Where we go, He goes. He can't get close to those who don't know His Spirit.

Beyond this, being yoked with other believers becomes a practical matter, a preventative medicine. No matter how much we feel we have in common with an unbeliever, those things are ultimately superficial. Down deep, we are different. We march to a completely different drummer; if we keep trying to march in step with unbelievers, we eventually will, and that brings about the pain of separation from God.

Living Out Those Guidelines Day after Day

If you have become close to an unbeliever, you may be digging in your heels at this point. You think you'll find a huge void in your life if you release that relationship, and the prospect is terrifying. But read on. The balance of chapter 6 is a series of promises, written in covenant-like language:

> Just as God said,
> "I will dwell in them and walk among them;
> And I will be their God, and they shall be My people.
> Therefore, come out from their midst and be separate," says the Lord.
> "And do not touch what is unclean;
> And I will welcome you.
> And I will be a father to you,
> And you shall be sons and daughters to Me,"
> Says the Lord Almighty. (vv. 16b–18)

God isn't asking you to be alone. In fact, He promises that you won't be. Did you notice all the relational words in this passage? In calling us to be separate from the world, He promises to comfort us with His presence. We will belong to Him, and He will belong to us. He'll welcome us, be like a father to us, and treat us like His own children. If we let Him, He can fill the hole in our hearts.

How, though, can we experience this?

Vertical Reverence

The first verse of chapter 7 goes on to tell us:

> Therefore, having these promises, beloved, let us cleanse ourselves from all defilement of flesh and spirit, perfecting holiness in the fear of God.

If we want to find contentment in the Lord, we have to put Him first. Worshiping the Lord should be our goal. But how do we show reverence for God? By making a clean break with defilement. By refusing to participate in anything that is unclean to the Lord, whether it's an activity, a relationship, or a way of thinking.

Does the word *perfecting* in that verse intimidate you? God isn't asking us to become perfect before He'll associate with us. The word *perfecting* in this context means "bringing to completion." Our holiness is a work in progress, an ongoing growth that comes when we submit to God and learn what pleases Him.

Horizontal Respect

Paul then transitioned from relationship with God to relationships with people—in this case, the Corinthians:

> Make room for us in your hearts; we wronged no one, we corrupted no one, we took advantage of no one. I do not speak to condemn you, for I have said before that you are in our hearts to die together and to live together. Great is my confidence in you; great is my boasting on your behalf. (vv. 2–4a)

Remember what Paul said back in 6:11–13? He had reached out to the Corinthians, and they had not reached back to him. Paul was returning to that issue, and in doing so, he made three statements about how we are to relate to each other.

First, *when we respect someone, we make room for them in our hearts*. It sounds like a deliberate action, doesn't it? Some people slide into our hearts with no effort at all. The fit is natural, the relationship easy. But others may have the potential to warm us, to teach us, and to give us great enjoyment; we may miss out on that blessing because we are consumed with our own lives or allow misunderstandings or misperceptions to bar the way. For those people, we need to "make room." We need to rearrange some of the furniture in our hearts to create a place for them. Imagine the treasures the Corinthians would have missed if they hadn't "made room" for Paul!

Second, *when we respect someone, we don't condemn them*. The Corinthians had thought and said some pretty negative things about Paul, and no doubt there were a few choice words he would have liked to say in response. But he restrained himself. Though he gently pointed out the faultiness of their thinking, he went to great lengths to balance his criticism with love and acceptance.

Third, *when we respect someone, we have confidence in them*. The Corinthians had made more than a few mistakes in carrying out their Christianity. But Paul believed in them, even when they failed. He stuck with them, encouraged them, and spurred them on to greatness.

Filled-to-Overflowing Benefits We Can Anticipate

The closing words of 7:4b hold two benefits that flow from Paul's prescription for relationships—comfort and joy.

> I am filled with comfort; I am overflowing with joy in all our affliction.

Don't you long to say that? Even amid all the trouble Paul faced in his personal life, his relationship with God and with the Corinthians gave him down-deep comfort, full-to-the-brim joy. Relationships will do that for you. They make you feel you can face anything. They even give you the courage to see trials for the friends that they really are. As Malcolm Muggeridge has said,

> Contrary to what might be expected, I look back on experiences that at the time seemed especially desolating and painful with particular satisfaction. Indeed, I can say with complete truthfulness that everything I have learned in my seventy-five years in this world, everything that has truly enhanced and enlightened my existence, has been through affliction and not through happiness, whether pursued or attained. In other words, if it ever were to be possible to eliminate affliction from our earthly existence by means of some drug or other medical mumbo jumbo . . . the result would not be to make life delectable, but to make it too banal and trivial to be endurable. This, of course, is what the Cross signifies. And it is the Cross, more than anything else, that has called me inexorably to Christ.[2]

Most people spend their lives trying to avoid pain and difficulty. But with Christ and the earthly relationships we are blessed with, we can face trials with peace, knowing that they only bring us closer to Him and closer to one another.

2. Malcolm Muggeridge, *A Twentieth Century Testimony* (Nashville, Tenn.: Thomas Nelson Publishers, 1978), pp. 72–73.

Living Insights

Have you ever wondered why your relationship with Christ didn't seem like enough? Why it didn't feel deep-down satisfying to you in a way that made you sufficiently secure to be selective in your other relationships?

If so, don't be too quick to shrug it off. Reread 2 Corinthians 6:17–18, and take note of the conditions God places on closeness with Him:

> "Therefore, come out from their midst and be
> separate," says the Lord.
> "And do not touch what is unclean;
> And I will welcome you.
> And I will be a father to you,
> And you shall be sons and daughters to Me,"
> Says the Lord Almighty.

If we want to find contentment in the Lord, we have to put Him first. We step toward that priority by separating ourselves from unhealthy ties with unbelievers and by making a clean break with ongoing sins in our lives.

Take a moment to reflect on how your life measures against those guidelines. Do your closest friendships meet the criteria Paul suggested for healthy relationships?

- Do you share an emotional bond? ____________________

____

____

____

____

- Are you linked by spiritual freedom? ____________________

____

____

____

____

Spend some time evaluating your activities and habits. Could any of them be considered "unclean"? What might you do to better "perfect holiness" in your life?

____

____

____

____

____

Our relationship with God affects our relationships with others, and our relationships with others affect our relationship with God. By taking care in who and what we bring into our lives, we bring ourselves that much closer to unity with God—and He gives us comfort and security as a result. So raise those guidelines and raise them high—your relationships will become more meaningful when you do!

Chapter 15

SINGIN' IN THE RAIN

2 Corinthians 7:1–7

Remember that line from the Carpenters' old song, "Rainy days and Mondays always get me down"? Sometimes it seems like life has a lot more rainy days and Mondays than sunny days and Sundays, doesn't it?

Maybe one of the reasons they tend to get us down is that they take us by surprise. We think life is supposed to be smooth-sailing and tough times should be the exception—but they're not. James said that "all kinds of trials and temptations crowd into [our] lives" (James 1:2 PHILLIPS).

Dr. Victor Frankl, who endured the Nazi holocaust developed a realistic acceptance of life's pain. He once wrote:

> The reason so many people are unhappy today and seeking help to cope with life is that they fail to understand what human existence is all about. Until we recognize that life is not just something to be enjoyed but rather is a *task* that each of us is assigned, we'll never find meaning in our lives and we'll never be truly happy.[1]

Sounds a lot like James' advice to not "resent [trials and temptations] as intruders, but welcome them as friends: (1:2 PHILLIPS), doesn't it? That is one of the greatest concepts we can ever embrace. Life is difficult, that's true. It's a task to be accomplished, and the rainy days come often and stay long. But life need not be bleak and grim.

The apostle Paul had quite a bit to say about his problems in his letters, yet you never get the idea that Paul was complaining about his hardships. He had a realistic perspective about them. He even found comfort in the midst of his troubles, a song of joy in the rhythm of the rain. How did he do it? Let's take a closer look at Paul's way of beating the blues.

1. As quoted by Charles R. Swindoll in *Three Steps Forward, Two Steps Back: Persevering through Pressure* (Nashville, Tenn.: Thomas Nelson Publishers, 1980), p. 182.

The Painful Rain

Earlier in our study, we discussed some of the troubles Paul faced in his ministry—beatings, imprisonment, tumults, labors, sleeplessness, and hunger (2 Cor. 6:5). But let's not forget the internal struggles he endured, too.

> For even when we came into Macedonia our flesh had no rest, but we were afflicted on every side: conflicts without, fears within. (7:5)

The word *fears* here comes from the Greek word *phobos*, from which we get our term *phobia*. It carries the idea of dread and panic, a shrinking from courage, the desire to run. Paul and his workers struggled against internal fear.

But perhaps even more difficult were the hurts that came from those Paul sought to serve. Verses 2–4a give us a hint of the mistrust the Corinthians evidently had toward him—as well as Paul's forgiving attitude in return:

> Make room for us in your hearts; we wronged no one, we corrupted no one, we took advantage of no one. I do not speak to condemn you, for I have said before that you are in our hearts to die together and to live together. Great is my confidence in you; great is my boasting on your behalf.

And as if that weren't enough, another kind of distress beset Paul as well. Verse 6 alludes to it:

> But God, who comforts the depressed, comforted us by the coming of Titus.

Not only was the apostle sprinkled with fears (v. 5), he was drenched with depression. All of us get depressed from time to time. Some depressions hover over us like a lingering cloud. Other types are more transitory, varying in degree and duration.

But many Christians deny their depression. They may feel that if they aren't positive and sunny all the time, they are letting Christ down. But by denying their depression, they deny reality. Just as every day isn't filled with sunshine, so our lives aren't continually filled with the radiance of Christ. We have to face the facts of darkness, long shadows, and rainy days in our lives.

The Joyful Song

The joyful song in Paul's life obviously didn't come from a lack of problems. In came in the midst of and in spite of the rain—"overflowing with joy *in* all our affliction" (7:4, emphasis added). He was comforted with the arrival of Titus, sent to him by God. And not only was Paul glad to see his friend, he was also happy to hear his news:

> And not only by his coming, but also by the comfort with which he was comforted in you, as he reported to us your longing, your mourning, your zeal for me; so that I rejoiced even more. (v. 7)

What was Titus' good news? That things in Corinth weren't as bad as Paul thought. They missed Paul. They were distressed by the difficulties he had experienced, and they were rooting for him.

You see, God was working through Paul's hardships to produce something precious in the Corinthian believers, and the apostle found joy in their progress. However, even if the Corinthians hadn't softened toward him, there was something about Paul's faith that would have given him joy anyway. To find that ingredient, we have to return to a verse we read in the previous lesson:

> Therefore, having these promises, beloved, let us cleanse ourselves from all defilement of flesh and spirit, perfecting holiness in the fear of God. (2 Cor. 7:1)

When we "fear God," when we hold Him in reverence and recognize who He is, we realize that nothing has entered our lives that He has not permitted. And because we know He loves us, we also know that each of these things has a purpose and that He will not abandon us in the midst of them. That promise can bring a ray of sun to any rainy day!

The Next Time It Rains

Between the lines of these verses are two secrets to singing during the rainy days of our lives. First, *denial of difficulties complicates our lives*. If we deny the rain, we also deny the warmth and comfort God wants to give us. Second, *resentment of the rain stunts our growth*. Remember what James said? "Don't resent [trials] as intruders, but welcome them as friends" (1:2 PHILLIPS). There are lessons to be learned in storms. There's maturity to be gained.

So, the next time it rains, don't put up an umbrella. Instead, stop, look, and listen. *Stop* feeling sorry for yourself or blaming others. *Look* for the lessons to be learned. *Listen* to the silent lyrics God is singing in your ear. And He will put a song in your heart, as He did for David:

> I waited patiently for the Lord;
> And He inclined to me and heard my cry.
> He brought me up out of the pit of destruction, out of the miry clay,
> And He set my feet upon a rock making my footsteps firm.
> He put a new song in my mouth, a song of praise to our God. (Ps. 40:1–3a)

Living Insights

God does indeed love us and have wonderful plans for our lives. But we'll still have days that get rained out. So, instead of giving you four spiritual laws, here are four spiritual *flaws* to look out for. If you can avoid these four misconceptions about the Christian life, your storms will be easier to deal with.

Flaw #1

When you become a Christian, all your problems are solved. The truth is, becoming a Christian complicates your life. For one thing, you immediately come into the realm of the spirit/flesh conflict that you hadn't experienced before.

Flaw #2

All the problems you will ever have are specifically addressed in the Bible. They aren't. Scripture does give us principles to guide us through any struggle, and God provides us with wise friends and counselors to help us. The Lord Himself sometimes shows us the way. But not all of our troubles will be addressed specifically in the Bible.

Flaw #3

If you're having problems, it is a sign that you are unspiritual. Problems certainly can be caused by sin, but some are simply a result of living in an imperfect world. Some are actually signs of positive spiritual activity—evidence that God is at work in us, refining and maturing us.

Flaw #4

Being exposed to sound Bible teaching automatically solves your problems. That's no more true than the idea that reading a map will transport you to Peru or that getting in the water will turn you into a fish!

Have any of these "flaws" been a source of confusion for you? Which misconceptions have caused you the most migraines?

____

____

____

____

What different perspectives do you have now?

____

____

____

____

What comfort can you gain from the way Paul handled his problems?

____

____

____

____

God uses rainy days to sprinkle us with His showers of affection and drench us in His love and comfort. Next time you find yourself in the midst of a storm, reach out for God's love to soothe you.

Chapter 16

REPROOFS THAT RESULT IN REPENTANCE

2 Corinthians 7:8–16

Wisdom. It's not the same as intelligence. It's different from street smarts and number smarts. It isn't even the knowledge and common sense that comes with age. Wisdom is *divine perception*—the ability to see life from God's point of view.

Paul elaborates on this definition in 1 Corinthians 2:

> And when I came to you, brethren, I did not come with superiority of speech or of wisdom, proclaiming to you the testimony of God. For I determined to know nothing among you except Jesus Christ, and Him crucified. I was with you in weakness and in fear and in much trembling, and my message and my preaching were not in persuasive words of wisdom, but in demonstration of the Spirit and of power, so that your faith would not rest on the wisdom of men, but on the power of God.
>
> Yet we do speak wisdom among those who are mature; a wisdom, however, not of this age nor of the rulers of this age, who are passing away. . . . Now we have received, not the spirit of the world, but the Spirit who is from God, so that we may know the things freely given to us by God, which things we also speak, not in words taught by human wisdom, but in those taught by the Spirit, combining spiritual thoughts with spiritual words. (vv. 1–6, 12–13)

According to these verses, wisdom is not something we're born with. It's not something we can glean from a book or a seminar. It comes from God, as James affirmed:

> But if any of you lacks wisdom, let him ask of God, who gives to all generously and without reproach, and it will be given to him. (1:5)

Proverbs, more than any other biblical book, is a storehouse of wisdom (1:1–6). Its main author, Solomon, personified wisdom by portraying it as a woman who cries out and begs us to listen:

> Wisdom shouts in the street,
> She lifts her voice in the square;
> At the head of the noisy streets she cries out;
> At the entrance of the gates in the city she utters her sayings:
> "How long, O naive ones, will you love being simple-minded?
> And scoffers delight themselves in scoffing
> And fools hate knowledge?" (1:20–22)

Did you notice the three kinds of people Wisdom addresses? Those who are naive, or simple; those who are gullible, easily deceived and enticed; and scoffers, who think they can get along without God and His advice. These people shrug off Wisdom's tap on their shoulder and do not listen for her voice.

Solomon went on to tell those of us who desire it where to find Wisdom:

> "Turn to my reproof,
> Behold, I will pour out my spirit on you;
> I will make my words known to you." (v. 23)

Reproof is another word for *rebuke*. It's God pointing out a fault or flaw. It's not comfortable—it's perhaps even painful—but if we listen, it produces wisdom.

In this last passage of our study, we're going to eavesdrop on a conversation between Paul and the Corinthians in which Paul referred to a reproof he had given them in an earlier letter. Before we do, though, let's first gain an appreciation for the value of correction.

Ancient Proverbs on Receiving God's Reproofs

How do we become people of wisdom? By learning from our mistakes, by being open to rebuke, by being quick to admit when we're wrong, and by receiving the well-intended wounds of a friend (Prov. 27:5–6). In chapter 19, we also learn how we may obtain wisdom:

> Strike a scoffer and the naive may become shrewd,
> But reprove one who has understanding and he will gain knowledge. . . .

> Cease listening, my son, to discipline,
> And you will stray from the words of knowledge.
> (vv. 25, 27)

We all know people who persistently refuse any form of criticism or even advice. Time and time again, we see them repeat their mistakes, and we shake our head and wonder, "What will it take to make them come to their senses? When are they ever going to learn?"

Unless they turn around and acknowledge their need, they never will. The only way to gain wisdom is to repent of what we've done wrong and submit to the One who knows a better way—like the Corinthians did.

A Lost Letter That Resulted in Repentance

In 2 Corinthians 7, we see the process of repentance at work:

> For though I caused you sorrow by my letter, I do not regret it; though I did regret it—for I see that that letter caused you sorrow, though only for a while. (v. 8)

Paul was referring to a letter he sent previously after he wrote 1 Corinthians, one that has been lost to our eyes. This missing epistle is sometimes referred to as the "Severe Letter" because in it Paul rebuked the Corinthians for continuing in sexual sin. After sending it, Paul had second thoughts about the pain he inflicted—much like some parents feel after spanking their errant child. Thankfully, after delivering the Severe Letter, Timothy returned to report the Corinthians' repentant spirit, which brought great relief to Paul (see vv. 6–7).

Just as the rod gives wisdom to a child (Prov. 29:15), so the sharp rap of rebuke on the spiritual knuckles of the Corinthians led to a change of heart:

> I now rejoice, not that you were made sorrowful, but that you were made sorrowful to the point of repentance; for you were made sorrowful according to the will of God, so that you might not suffer loss in anything through us. For the sorrow that is according to the will of God produces a repentance without regret, leading to salvation, but the sorrow of the world produces death. (2 Cor. 7:9–10)

The difference between the sorrow inflicted by God and the sorrow inflicted by the world is that one is purposeful while the other is pointless. Sorrow according to the will of God is not an end in itself; it is a means to an end. It is redemptive—nothing is lost, only gained (see Rom. 8:28).

What makes suffering remedial is not its pain but our reaction to it. A reaction of repentance opens the door to wisdom. A reaction of resentment bolts the door against an opportunity to learn from the experience.

Almost all rebuke causes us discomfort. Sometimes it even causes us to be sorry—but not necessarily for what we've done. We may only be sorry that we've been caught! How can you recognize true repentance when you see it? Look at this checklist:

> For behold what *earnestness* this very thing, this godly sorrow, has produced in you: what *vindication* of yourselves, what *indignation*, what *fear*, what *longing*, what *zeal*, what *avenging of wrong!* In everything you demonstrated yourselves to be innocent in the matter. (2 Cor. 7:11, emphasis added)

Repentance is recognized by its results.

The Corinthians were fortunate to have a friend like Paul who was not afraid to wound them with the truth—a friend who loved them enough to point out their failings. We all need a friend like that . . . a friend like the one Solomon described in Proverbs 27:6:

> Faithful are the wounds of a friend,
> But deceitful are the kisses of an enemy.

Most of us have friends with whom we can discuss spiritual things. But how many of those friends do we really get personal with? How many know us well enough to see our flaws and open our eyes to them?

God knows us best, of course—warts and all. And He'd love to help us excise them, if we'll only give Him permission. David's prayer in Psalm 139 is a good example:

> Search me, O God, and know my heart;
> Try me and know my anxious thoughts;
> And see if there be any hurtful way in me,
> And lead me in the everlasting way. (vv. 23–24)

Back in 2 Corinthians 7, Paul reminded the Corinthians that

their mistake had done more than just the obvious damage—it had also created a rift between them and Paul. And their repentance had not only corrected the initial problem but had healed the relational hurt as well:

> So although I wrote to you, it was not for the sake of the offender nor for the sake of the one offended, but that your earnestness on our behalf might be made known to you in the sight of God. For this reason we have been comforted. (v. 12–13a)

While we often think we sin in secret, our mistakes are seldom contained in one area. They have far-reaching effects, and so does our repentance.

Perhaps the clearest teaching in the Bible on the subject of repentance can be found in Hebrews 12:5–11:

> You have forgotten the exhortation which is addressed to you as sons,
>
> "My son, do not regard lightly the discipline of the Lord,
> Nor faint when you are reproved by Him;
> For those whom the Lord loves He disciplines,
> And He scourges every son whom He receives."
>
> It is for discipline that you endure; God deals with you as with sons; for what son is there whom his father does not discipline? But if you are without discipline, of which all have become partakers, then you are illegitimate children and not sons. Furthermore, we had earthly fathers to discipline us, and we respected them; shall we not much rather be subject to the Father of spirits, and live? For they disciplined us for a short time as seemed best to them, but He disciplines us for our good, so that we may share His holiness. All discipline for the moment seems not to be joyful, but sorrowful; yet to those who have been trained by it, afterwards it yields the peaceful fruit of righteousness.

Have you ever disciplined your child and then had him fling himself in your arms, sobbing, "I'm sorry, Daddy!"? That's what Hebrews 12 is all about. That's the "afterwards" of it all. That's the "peaceful fruit of righteousness" that comes when we throw ourselves on the mercy of God—He embraces us in loving arms, forgiving us fully.

Conflict produces anxiety (2 Cor. 2:4), but reproof leading to repentance can resolve conflict and bring peace. And when conflict is resolved, a flood of good things rushes into the relationship:

> And besides our comfort, we rejoiced even much more for the joy of Titus, because his spirit has been refreshed by you all. For if in anything I have boasted to him about you, I was not put to shame; but as we spoke all things to you in truth, so also our boasting before Titus proved to be the truth. His affection abounds all the more toward you, as he remembers the obedience of you all, how you received him with fear and trembling. I rejoice that in everything I have confidence in you. (7:13b–16)

Comfort, rejoicing, refreshment . . . affirmation, knowledge of the truth, confidence . . . affection, obedience, acceptance . . . more rejoicing and greater confidence. What a change from the tension that existed before! And all because a reproof was heeded.

Remember where we started? If we want to become wise, we need to heed God's reproofs. But look at all the side benefits that come as well!

Timely Reminders Regarding Reproofs and Repentance

First, *godlike wisdom is still available, but without reproof it remains distant.* Wisdom from God comes in packages, some in the form of reproof. And each is opened by means of repentance.

Second, *God's reproofs come in many ways, but they fall flat without repentance.* From whom do these packages of reproof come? From parents, from children, from teachers, coaches, and counselors. From friends, from coworkers, from failures. From Scripture, from sickness. By letter, by loss, by disaster, by disappointment. They come in all shapes and sizes, but all require repentance.

Third, *godly repentance unlocks the door, but only one can enter at a time.* God deals with each of us individually; when we come through Wisdom's door, we have to walk in single file. It's a door that's open to you right now. Won't you leave your pride on the porch and come inside?

Living Insights

Rebuke is always a tough pill to swallow—maybe because it always gets washed down with pride!

Take a minute to humble yourself before God, praying the same prayer David prayed in Psalm 139:23–24:

> Search me, O God, and know my heart;
> Try me and know my anxious thoughts;
> And see if there be any hurtful way in me,
> And lead me in the everlasting way.

Now, spend some time listening to God, and write down anything He reveals in your life that is worrisome or destructive.

How do you respond to that reproof?

God's reproofs are painful for a moment, but their effects are positive and rewarding. They make us more like Christ, and they draw us closer to His side.

Second Corinthians offers a kaleidoscope of themes to reflect on: suffering, integrity, forgiveness, death, reverence, reproof. All are part of a colorful but fragmentary picture of Paul's ministry to the Corinthians.

As we turn these varicolored flecks over in our minds, new light shines on our own circumstances. Through Paul's pain, we gain perspective. Through his struggles, we gain the strength to persevere. Through his firm yet tender admonitions, we gain a whole new respect for relationships. When we apply Paul's response to ministry to our own lives, ministry becomes deeper, stronger, and more colorful with each passing day.

Books for Probing Further

The following books will help bring into focus many of the themes Paul touched on only briefly in his heartfelt letter to the Corinthians. Together they form a mosaic of a ministry anyone could trust.

Augsburger, David. *The Freedom of Forgiveness*. Revised and expanded. Chicago, Ill.: Moody Press, 1988.

Haugk, Kenneth C. *Antagonists in the Church: How to Identify and Deal with Destructive Conflict*. Minneapolis, Minn.: Augsburg Fortress Publishers, 1988.

Hughes, Kent and Barbara Hughes. *Liberating Ministry from the Success Syndrome*. Wheaton, Ill.: Tyndale House, 1992.

Hughes, Philip Edgcumbe. *Paul's Second Epistle to the Corinthians*. Grand Rapids, Mich.: William B. Eerdmans Publishing Co., 1962.

Peterson, Eugene H. *Working the Angles*. Grand Rapids, Mich.: William B. Eerdmans Publishing Co., 1987.

VanVonderen, Jeffrey. *When God's People Let You Down: How to Rise Above Hurts that Often Occur Within the Church*. Minneapolis, Minn.: Bethany House, 1995.

Wilson, Earl, Sandra Wilson, and Nancy Paulson. *Restoring the Fallen: A Team Approach to Caring, Confronting, and Reconciling*. Downers Grove, Ill.: InterVarsity Press, 1997.

Yancey, Philip. *Disappointment with God*. Grand Rapids, Mich.: Zondervan Publishing House, 1988.

Some of the books listed may be out of print and available only through a library. For those currently available, please contact your local Christian bookstore. Books by Charles R. Swindoll may be obtained through the Insight for Living Resource Center, as well as many books by other authors. Just call the IFL office that serves you.

Insight for Living also has Bible study guides available on many books of the Bible as well as on a variety of topics, Bible characters, and contemporary issues. For more information, see the ordering instructions that follow and contact the office that serves you.

Notes

Notes

Notes

NOTES

ORDERING INFORMATION

A MINISTRY ANYONE COULD TRUST

If you would like to order additional Bible study guides, purchase the audiocassette series that accompanies this guide, or request our product catalogs, please contact the office that serves you.

United States and International locations:

Insight for Living
Post Office Box 269000
Plano, TX 75026-9000

1-800-772-8888, 24 hours a day, seven days a week (U.S. contacts)
International constituents may contact the U.S. office through mail queries.

Canada:

Insight for Living Ministries
Post Office Box 2510
Vancouver, BC, Canada V6B 3W7

1-800-663-7639, 24 hours a day, seven days a week
InfoCanada@insight.org

Australia:

Insight for Living, Inc.
20 Albert Street
Blackburn, VIC 3130, Australia

Toll-free 1800 772 888 or (03) 9877-4277, 8:30 A.M. to 5:00 P.M., Monday to Friday
iflaus@insight.org

World Wide Web:
www.insight.org

Bible Study Guide Subscription Program

Bible study guide subscriptions are available. Please call or write the office nearest you to find out how you can receive our Bible study guides on a regular basis.